ON GUILT
AND INNOCENCE

On Guilt
and Innocence

*Essays in Legal Philosophy
and Moral Psychology*

Herbert Morris

UNIVERSITY OF CALIFORNIA PRESS

Berkeley • Los Angeles • London

University of California Press
Berkeley and Los Angeles, California
University of California Press, Ltd.
London, England
Copyright © 1976 by
The Regents of the University of California
First Paperback Printing 1979
ISBN 0-520-03944-0
Library of Congress Catalog Card Number: 72-89789
Printed in the United States of America

1 2 3 4 5 6 7 8 9

Contents

Preface

EACH of the essays in this volume, all but the last having been published before, deals in some way with those common human experiences in which individuals deliberately inflict pain upon others or upon themselves because of a judgment of guilt or forbear from its infliction because of a judgment of innocence. These are familiar practices, within and outside the law, but no human behavior has generated greater scepticism and greater disagreement than that which invokes the distinction between guilt and innocence and which visits pain upon the guilty.

Philosophers have, of course, written exhaustively on the themes of punishment and responsibility. They have asked what it is to punish and whether this practice is justifiable, and, if so, for what reasons. They have puzzled over a host of questions connected with responsibility, ranging from the so-called "free will versus determinism" dispute to an examination of the principles applicable in everyday life to ascriptions of responsibility. In the voluminous literature on these topics remarkably little attention has been paid to the concepts of guilt and guilt feelings, and, apart from work on conscience, to the rich assortment of related concepts such as remorse, repentance, contrition, forgiveness, and shame. The complex world of moral feelings, a world so central to our lives, so deep in significance for us, so vividly and thoroughly displayed in literature, has attracted about as little attention from philosophers as the world of responsibility before Austin's "A Plea for Excuses." In these essays there is an attempt to rectify this philosophical neglect. A better grasp of guilt and related concepts will mean a more informed judgment of the merits of our common moral and legal practices. It will mean, too—if the author's hopes are at least partially realized—a deeper understanding of ourselves and of our conception of the world.

Serious consideration is given not merely to neglected topics but to paradoxical claims, claims that have met with scorn in addition to neglect. Recurrently espoused views—views held by only a few—that appear on their face to be false, even nonsensical, are treated with respect. What motivates this is not, at least entirely, a strange fascination for the outlandish or a perverse satisfaction in championing against the horde the outcast and underdog. It is the view that philosophical criticism achieves more of what we should all wish for it when it attempts to grasp some perception people have been struggling—often ineptly and frustratingly—to convey than by resting content citing obvious inadequacies. These essays are marked by a principle of tolerance because of the belief that in philosophy, as in poetry, what appears false or nonsensical often hides an, as yet, unexpressed insight.

The first essay, "Punishment for Thoughts," attempts to explain and then to defend the ridiculed claim, one that seems to fly in the face of moral and legal experience, that "law is concerned with external conduct; morality with internal conduct." What is it to punish for thought alone? What is it, if anything, that proscribes the law making criminal thought alone and punishing for it? These are two large questions examined in this essay.

In "Persons and Punishment" the striking claim is put forward—some may consider it absurd—that we have a right to be punished.

The claim is defended by constructing and then comparing two different models of human behavior and responses to deviant conduct. One is the model of human responsibility and punishment for wrongdoing, the other a model of all deviance as pathological behavior calling for a response of control or therapy. I have included three brief essays as addenda to "Persons and Punishment." The first treats modes of response to human conduct that are neither punitive nor therapeutic as these have been defined in the principal essay. There is, principally, an examination of shame and how it contrasts with guilt and there is an explanation of the peculiar fittingness of the concept of guilt to law. The second addendum is a critical discussion of the work of Thomas Szasz whose claim that there is no such thing as mental illness conflicts with a central assumption of "Persons and Punishment." The third essay is a critical review of Herbert Fingarette's *The Meaning of Criminal Insanity*, one of the very few attempts by a philosopher to offer an analysis of what it is to be insane.

"Guilt and Suffering" is addressed to the important conflict between those who claim that guilt feelings are rational and those who claim that they are not. The one group believes that were we in some manner to lose our liability to this feeling we should in some important way become deformed as human beings. The other group finds any feeling, even when not neurotic, that disposes one to inflict suffering because of what is past and irretrievable, with an unconcern for the future, unjustifiable because pointless infliction of pain. There are analyses of guilt, guilt feelings, and connections that these feelings have with pain and suffering. In the final section the author indicates his own reservations about guilt.

"Shared Guilt" investigates the truth that may lie behind the view sympathetically presented by Dostoyevsky in *The Brothers Kara-mazov*—"we are responsible for everything."

Finally, "Lost Innocence," using the tale of Adam and Eve as a springboard for philosophical inquiry, examines an obviously significant human experience entirely neglected by philosophers and left by them, without explanation, for literary artists and theologians.

Acknowledgment with thanks is made for the use of the following essays: "Punishment for Thoughts": reprinted from *The Monist*, vol. 49, no. 3 (July 1965); "Persons and Punishment": reprinted from *The Monist*, vol. 52, no. 4 (October 1968); "Guilt and Punishment": reprinted from *The Personalist*, vol. 52, no. 2 (1971); "Szasz: The Manufacture of Madness": reprinted from 18 *UCLA Law Review*, 1164-72 (1971); "Criminal Insanity": reprinted from *Inquiry*, 17 (1974), 345-355; "Guilt and Suffering": reprinted from *Philosophy East and West*, 21, 4 (1971), 419-434; "Shared Guilt": reprinted from *Wisdom: Twelve Essays* (Oxford: Basil H. Blackwell, 1974).

H. M.

1 Punishment
for Thoughts

THOSE who attempt to answer the question "What is the
nature of law?" or the question "What is the nature of morality?"
often also consider how law and morality are related. When they
do this, they tend to give answers that emphasize differences rather
than likenesses. They are interested, however, in not just any
differences but in those that are "essential." Most believe that there
is *one* such difference. They often express this in a "formula" or
"maxim" that sums up their views both on law and morality and on
the essential difference between them.[1]

The most famous and perhaps the most obscure of these
formulae is: "Law is concerned with external conduct; morality
with internal conduct." Short work has sometimes been made of
this proposal.[2] If the claim is, as it is sometimes taken to be, that the
law is concerned exclusively with conduct and morality exclusively
with states of mind, it is only necessary to point out that states of
mind are relevant to the law and conduct is relevant to morality.

Reprinted from *The Monist* (July 1965).

The definitions of burglary and murder, to take two obvious examples, demonstrate that states of mind are relevant to law. And conduct seems relevant to morality, for we blame people for telling lies, breaking promises, killing people, not just, or perhaps ever, for merely contemplating, desiring, or intending to do these things. What, then, is left of the view that law is concerned with external conduct and morality with internal conduct?

The ease of this refutation may produce a vague disquiet, a feeling that perhaps the point of the maxim has escaped the critic. Could those philosophers who have thought it true been oblivious to these facts about our moral and legal life to which appeal is made in refuting it? The facts seem too obvious to be overlooked. It is reasonable to suppose that philosophers who have thought in terms of the external-internal distinction were getting at something.

This is the view adopted by other philosophers. They are in agreement that the maxim is obscure, but they think that it contains some important insight into the nature of law and morals. Stammler writes that we are given "only a suggestion of a difference."[3] Radbruch writes of "concealed" meanings.[4] Kantorowicz believes we must maintain the distinction provided that it is "rightly understood."[5] Hart believes that "though it contains a hint of truth it is, as it stands, profoundly misleading."[6] When the truth hinted at is brought into the open, these critics turn out to be not wholly in agreement on what is hidden. In some cases there are clear differences of opinion as to the truth it contains. In some cases what is proposed as an implication of the maxim seems to have little connection with it; the use of the words "external" and "internal" has simply called something to mind.

It seems to me, too, that there may be some truth in the formula. My aim in this paper is (1) to offer an interpretation of the formula; (2) to examine one limited aspect of it that relates to law; and (3) to offer a defense of this limited aspect.

There are at least three points that a philosopher committed to the view that "law is concerned with external conduct, morality with internal conduct" may wish to make:

a. Law requires external conduct. In morality one may be blamed or praised for one's mental state alone; there are sins and virtues of thought.
b. In law, conduct by itself is sufficient to constitute compliance with rules. In morality conduct alone is never sufficient.
c. In law, conduct alone is (or may be) sufficient to create liability. In morality one may never be blamed for conduct alone.

Each of these claims about law and about morality is, as it stands, obscure, suggestive and worth, I think, examining in some detail. That would be a large undertaking. In this paper my goal is relatively modest. I restrict inquiry to the first claim that law requires external conduct. I restrict myself still further by interpreting the claim as one made about the criminal law. When the word "law" occurs, then, it should be understood as meaning "the criminal law."

There are at least two sources of obscurity with respect to the claim. First, if someone says, "for law there must be external conduct," we may be unsure what would and what would not satisfy this demand. Does the philosopher mean, for example, that punishment for omitting to do something is, in some sense, unacceptable? Second, we may be unsure whether or not the cases that come readily to mind as possible counterinstances have relevance to the claim, not because, as with omissions, we are unsure what class of things would count for or against the claim, but because we are unsure about the status of the claim. By this I mean we may be unsure what procedures, if any, are appropriate for confirming or disconfirming the claim. Is it a factual claim or a moral claim or some other kind of claim? Does it make any difference to its validity, for example, that a statute has been enacted in accord with law that makes it an offense to intend to commit arson? We must look more carefully at each of these sources of obscurity if we are to settle whether or not this limited aspect of the maxim is valid. Let us turn to the first source of obscurity.

I

Among the things a philosopher may mean when he says "law is concerned with external conduct" is "for law there must be conduct." If he means this, he is claiming not, as it is sometimes supposed he is, that law is exclusively concerned with conduct, a position that appears obviously untenable, but rather that law is not concerned with states of mind alone, a position that is not obviously untenable. What, then, would it be like for the law to be concerned with a state of mind alone?

In the remainder of this part of the paper I shall attempt to clarify the relationship between conduct and mental states in a variety of legal situations so that we have a better grasp of the kind of case to be ruled out by the philosopher's claim "for the law there must be conduct."

1. Suppose that it is made a punishable offense *to disbelieve* the story of creation as recorded in the Old Testament. Suppose, further, that an admission in open court is required for conviction and that such an admission by itself is sufficient for conviction of the offense. Here we have a clear case of a law concerned with a state of mind alone. What are some of its features? First, the offense is defined exclusively in psychological terms. Second, an admission without any accompanying conduct is sufficient to convict a person for the offense. Third, there is no interest the law seeks to protect that is threatened by the admission, thus there is nothing paradoxical in the law's seeking to encourage the admission. Fourth, the law is prohibiting a state of mind. Fifth, in prohibiting a state of mind the object of the law is merely to induce persons not to have a state of mind, and we shall assume that the law's aim is not thereby to prevent some harm related to the state of mind.

A person who understood this law would realize that he had committed an offense when he disbelieved the story of creation. He would understand that to admit disbelief was not to commit an offense but merely to reveal its commission. It is natural to say in such a case that a person punished for committing this offense is being punished for thought alone and hence that the law was concerned with a state of mind alone.[7]

2. Our first case may suggest that one is punished for thought

alone if one is punished for committing an offense defined exclusively in psychological terms. I am not sure that this criterion will do. Suppose persons possessed the capacity to arouse fear in other persons merely by thinking in a particular way. Suppose that it were a punishable offense to arouse fear in others by exercising this capacity. It is at least arguable that this is an offense defined exclusively in psychological terms. Punishment for committing the offense, however, would not be for thought alone but for arousing fear by thought. From this it follows: (a) that some offenses may be defined exclusively in psychological terms and yet there be "external conduct" and (b) that there may be "external conduct" even though an offense may be committed without a person's doing anything that involves a bodily movement.

3. There is another reason why it is undesirable to restrict "external conduct" to conduct that involves a bodily movement. It is, of course, understandable that we should think of external conduct in terms of bodily movements. A philosopher who says "there must be external conduct" contrasts external conduct with what is misleadingly labeled "internal conduct," that is, with mental states, such as beliefs, desires, wishes, and intentions. This seems clear enough. If we then ask what is meant by "external conduct," it seems reasonable to suggest that it means "a physical act or acts," for we often contrast the physical with the mental. If we then ask "what is a physical act?" the response, no doubt, will be that it is or involves a bodily movement. If we then turn attention again to the claim, "there must be external conduct," it looks as if it is being claimed that there cannot be a legal offense or there cannot be punishment unless there is some bodily movement. But now a difficulty presents itself. When we hold a person liable for an omission we do not hold him liable only on condition that he has moved his body. We may, then, wonder how omissions are accommodated by the philosopher's statement and conclude that they are not. Rules which require persons to do things would, in some sense, be unacceptable to the philosopher.

If, when we say "there must be external conduct," we intend merely to rule out punishment for thought alone, it is strange to rule out omissions, for this would suggest that a person punished for omitting to pay taxes was being punished for thought alone. And this, of course, is not so. Suppose, however, that we were legally required to have certain thoughts. Punishment for omitting to have the thoughts would be punishment for thought alone. One reaches the conclusion that omissions are not external conduct only by identifying external conduct with bodily movements and interpreting one who claims "there must be external conduct" as claiming that there is no legal offense without bodily movement, whereas the aim behind the remark, I believe, is to preclude punishment merely for having or not having a certain mental state. Omissions then may or may not, depending on whether it is an omission to act or to think, be "external conduct" within the meaning of this phrase as employed by one who insists that law cannot punish for thought alone.

4. Suppose that it were a punishable offense *to intend* to assassinate a public official. Suppose, on analogy with the evidential requirement for conviction of treason,[8] that an evidential rule required, for conviction, that evidence be introduced that the accused took substantial steps toward assassinating a public official. In these circumstances, the class of those who may be convicted of *intending* to assassinate a public official may coincide with the class of those who may be convicted of *attempting* to assassinate a public official, for attempting may be defined as intending to perform some act and taking substantial steps in furtherance of one's intention. Now, if the philosopher would not object to punishment for attempts, would he object to the offense that we have imagined? There are grounds, I think, for believing that he would regard punishment under these circumstances as punishment for thought alone.

Suppose, first, a very unusual situation. The law's *sole* interest in or concern with the substantial steps might be evidential. If this were so, the law might even encourage those steps that reveal the intention. We could, in fact, understand the law providing inducements to persons to do all that they could to realize their intentions, for such behavior would provide the best evidence of one's intending to assassinate a public official. In these circumstances the law would be seeking to prevent what it prohibits and nothing else. If one were punished in such a case it would not be *for* acting any more than it was *for* admitting in our case of disbelief in the story of creation. While conduct is a prerequisite for conviction it is not *for conduct* that the person is being punished.

Clearly, the more realistic case is one in which there is a different attitude toward the conduct insisted upon by the evidential rule. In prohibiting an intention to assassinate a public official we naturally would be aiming at diminishing the number of such assassinations. And if this is so, it would be absurd to encourage the conduct that provides evidence of intention. Two preliminary questions are raised by such an offense where the concern with conduct is not exclusively evidential. First, what is the point of the evidential requirement? Second, why are the substantial steps not a defining element of the offense?

First, it is understandable that there should be such an evidential requirement. A balance is always struck between the aims of convicting the guilty and avoiding the conviction of the innocent. While fewer guilty persons will be convicted if we require substantial steps, rather than a mere confession, there will also be fewer innocent persons convicted. Persons innocent of intending might confess to intending for any number of reasons, but, so the theory might be, fewer of those innocent of intending would take substantial steps toward assassinating a public official.

Second, if in this system one may be punished for the separate crime of "intending to assassinate a public official and taking substantial steps in furtherance of one's intention," that is, for attempting to assassinate a public official, what is the point of the additional offense of merely intending? To answer this question we must look at this law from the point of view of one seeking to comply with legal rules. The offense of intending to assassinate a public official may operate to disincline persons from forming such intentions. It may lead to an exercise of self-restraint at a stage earlier than a law with respect to attempts. I shall have some more comments on this explanation later on, but for the moment I propose we accept it.[9]

What shall we say about whether or not punishment for such an offense is punishment for thought alone? There are two respects in which conduct is relevant here that it was not in the case of disbelief in the story of creation. Conduct, apart from admissions, is insisted upon by an evidential rule. And it is harmful conduct and not merely an intention that we are, by hypothesis, seeking to diminish by making the intention wrongful. But these differences do not warrant concluding that this is a case in which we are punishing for something apart from thought. First, the status of the conduct in the evidential rule is like that of the admission in our case of disbelief. Conduct simply affords more reliable evidence than a mere admission of the state made illegal. But this is not relevant to what it is that one is being punished for. Second, from the fact that we are interested in prohibiting intentions in order to diminish certain harm it does not follow that we punish, not for intentions, but for conduct or for harm. If we punish a person, for example, for behaving recklessly, in the absence of actual harm, we punish for his reckless conduct although our ultimate aim may be to diminish a type of harm the risk of which is increased by the reckless conduct. We must distinguish between *what* it is we are punishing *for* and *why* it is that we are punishing.

5. Suppose we had a device for detecting sincere confessions. Would we then seek to punish persons who intended to assassinate public officials but who, subsequent to intending and before taking steps, changed their minds? If our purpose is to prevent harm, what, we might wonder, is to be served by punishing such persons? Someone may then suggest that we should be interested not in mere intentions but in firm ones. Let us, then, suppose it is a punishable offense "to have the *firm intention* to assassinate a public official." Suppose an evidential requirement similar to the one we have been considering. Would punishment for this offense be for thought alone? What is "firm intention?"

Perhaps a "firm intention" is to be contrasted with a state of indecision. If one's mind is made up, one's intention is firm or fixed.

But is it, then, clear what "an intention" that is not firm might be? It may be that "firm" is to be contrasted with "weak" rather than with "not yet definite." "Firmness" would be a function of one's beliefs and feelings with regard to a change of mind. If, for example, a person believes that nothing will dissuade him from seeking to realize his intention and if his feelings are strong on the matter, his intention may be regarded as firm. If he believes that only extraordinary circumstances will make him change his mind and feels rather strongly, then his intention may be considered only relatively firm. If he is prepared to change his mind at any moment and for almost any reason, he may be considered merely to intend. Given the law's aim to strike some balance between preventing harm and not interfering with those who will do no harm, one could understand the law's drawing a distinction between those who intend and those who firmly intend. The latter are more likely to invade interests protected by law. Still, for the reasons offered in the preceding case, a person would be punished for thought alone if punished for this state of mind whatever our ultimate object in punishing such persons.

6. Sometimes firm intention is used interchangeably with another phrase, "firm resolve" or "constancy of purpose," and this suggests another situation.[10] Suppose it were a punishable offense "to have the *firm resolve* to assassinate a public official." Suppose, again, the evidential requirement. Now what class of persons interests us here? It is a class of persons that, by hypothesis, differs from those who intend and those who firmly intend as we have understood these phrases. This class may be described as the class of those "who really intend" or the class of those whose "purpose is constant." Let us attempt to clarify this concept.

In those cases in which intention and firm intention were made criminal, it did not seem particularly difficult to understand what state it was we were not to have in order to conform to the law. It was assumed that a person could have the state in question, realize that he had it, and realize that his conduct served merely to reveal his inner state to others. Were we to have a machine that could reliably test when one was sincerely reporting his state of mind, such a machine would allow us to determine whether or not one intended or firmly intended even in the absence of conduct in furtherance of intention.[11] What shall we say of "firm resolve"? This phrase may be introduced to cover the following situation. We may believe that a person was sincere in expressing an intention, sincere in expressing a firm intention and yet not believe that he "really intended" or that "his resolve was firm" or that "his purpose was constant." We might hold such beliefs if, when the occasion arrived for the person doing what he said he intended to do, he did nothing. When "the chips were down" he didn't come through as he said he intended to. Now someone may say that law should be restricted to those who firmly resolve, to those who "really intend." But what, then, does "firm resolve" imply?

It seems to me that conduct is related to "firm resolve" in a way unlike we took it to be related to intending and firmly intending. In those cases we viewed conduct merely as a sign of the intention. With "firm resolve," however, the conduct is not only a sign of the intention or resolve but part of the meaning of "firm." If a person, for whatever reason, does not do what he believes necessary to realize his intention one cannot say his resolve was firm. Lie-detecting devices might come to be accepted as reliable guides to intention and firm intention, but hardly for "firm resolve" as I am construing it. For "firm" implies that the person does what he believes necessary to realize his resolve.[12] To detect "firm resolve," then, we would need a device that could foretell the future. But now, if "firm resolve" implies more than merely having a certain mental state, what is it that persons are to avoid doing if they are to comply with the law making it criminal to have a firm resolve to assassinate a public official? What does the law direct persons not to do? It must be to avoid *acting* with a certain state of mind. But if this is so, are we prohibiting a state of mind by itself?

The topic of "firm resolve" leads to the next major problem in understanding what constitutes "punishment for thought alone." Sometimes it is suggested that a person is punished for thought alone despite the fact that the offense he has committed is defined partly in physical terms. Laws, for example, with respect to conspiracy, vagrancy, and possession of burglar's tools may occasion such an observation.[13] It is most often made about the law of attempts.[14]

It has been claimed that the sole purpose for requiring conduct in the law of attempts is to establish the *mens rea*. This assimilates the conduct requirement in such laws to the evidential status of conduct in our earlier cases of intention and firm intention. Such claims are misleading. But showing why this is so does not settle the issue whether or not we punish for thoughts alone when we punish for attempts. I want first to suggest three reasons why conduct is an element of the offense.[15]

First, crimes of attempt allow enforcement officials to prevent both those who have set out to commit crimes from consummating them and those who failed to consummate crimes through some accident or mistake from trying again. The law of attempts enables enforcement officials to interfere with individuals before any harm has been done so that harm may be prevented. This power to interfere, however, is circumscribed. While we wish to protect individuals against theft and murder we also wish to protect individuals against interference by the state if these individuals, whatever their state of mind, would not in fact commit crimes. There is a point, an ill-defined one, at which the risk of harm to interests the law seeks to protect becomes so great that it is thought desirable to interfere with individuals who might change their minds. Now at what point does the law decide that that interference is worth the risk of penalizing those who would change their minds? Those who claim the sole purpose of requiring conduct is to establish the *mens rea* seem to imply that the law would if sufficiently reliable evidence were available, interfere with those who intend or firmly intend to commit crimes. And, indeed, there might be some justification for such a viewpoint, for it is probably the case that individuals with such states of mind are more likely than the general run of persons to act to realize their intentions and invade the interests of others protected by law. But if our ultimate aim is to balance the policy of preventing harm to persons with the policy of minimizing interference with those who would not do all they believe necessary to realize their intentions, then the law may insist upon conduct because, comparing the class of those who firmly intend with the class of those who firmly intend and who take steps to realize their intentions, members of the former class are more likely than those of the latter to change their minds. In drawing the line at "performing the proximate act" the law assures that fewer of those who would change their minds are convicted although it also thereby, of course, assumes a greater risk that the sphere of protected interests will be invaded.

Second, a person who takes steps in furtherance of his intention to commit a crime may be regarded as more disposed than the general run of persons to criminal activity generally. It is understandable that we may wish to have control over such persons in order to apply whatever corrective measures are thought beneficial. Those who intend to commit crimes, those who firmly intend to commit crimes, those who take steps to realize their intentions are all more disposed to criminal activity than the general run of persons. But it is also the case that those who take steps in furtherance of their intentions are more disposed toward criminal activity than those who do not take steps to realize their intentions. It is reasonable and compatible with the definition of the offense of attempt that the law draw a line guided by this consideration so that those who take no steps are excluded from liability.

Third, were we to exculpate individuals who attempted to commit crimes but failed, say, through some fortuity, there would be an inequality of treatment of persons who were equally guilty from a moral point of view. Now, if we consider the class of persons who intend, the class of those who firmly intend, the class of those who take steps to realize their intentions, and the class of those who take the last step necessary to realize their intentions, we may regard them all as more morally blameworthy than the general run of persons. But they are not equally so. Those who take the last step are, in general, as blameworthy as those who succeed. Those who take the "proximate step" may, of course, change their minds before the last step, but as we have seen, they are less likely than the general run of persons who intend to commit crimes to do so. Because of this it is less likely that they differ significantly in blameworthiness from those who actually commit the crime.

It might be admitted that the foregoing was a fairly adequate explanation of why the offense is defined in physical terms and still be maintained that when a person is punished for attempting to commit a crime he is being punished *for* his state of mind alone and not for what he has done. What he has done may be harmless, and it cannot be for what is harmless that we are punishing him.

In assessing this view it is advisable, I think, to distinguish those attempt situations in which the individual has done all he believes necessary to realize his intention and fails for one reason or another and those in which, while he has taken substantial steps in furtherance of his intention, he has not yet taken the last step he believes necessary to realize his intention. Let us consider the first class of attempts.

Here it is surely strange to say that we are punishing for a state of mind alone. If we view the situation as it actually exists, a particular person held liable for an attempt may have done no harm. We can hardly, however, infer from this that we are punishing such a person for his state of mind alone. This would suggest that we are punishing him for precisely what we would be punishing a person for if mere or firm intention were made criminal. The natural thing to say for this class of attempts is that we are punishing the person for doing all that he believes necessary to accomplish his intention. The person has engaged in conduct with a certain state of mind and the law has deemed that that conduct with that state of mind creates risks the law seeks to diminish. From the fact that one who drives recklessly is punished in the absence of harm one cannot, as we have seen, legitimately infer that the person is not being punished for reckless driving. Such conduct creates risks of harm and though it may not in a particular case result in harm the law may seek to diminish the risk. Likewise, persons who perform all they believe necessary to achieve their intentions generally do succeed, which suggests that in conducting themselves as they do, these persons create serious risk of harm.

The more interesting case is that of attempts in which the last step has not been taken. Are we not in such cases punishing for a state of mind alone? It is seriously misleading to say we are. It may suggest that were lie-detecting devices regarded as reliable, admissions of intentions, tested by such devices, would provide precisely what substantial steps now provide us in attempted crimes. And this is mistaken, I think, for several reasons. First, it cannot be disputed that one may intend to commit a crime and provide reliable evidence of one's intention and not be guilty of attempt. In attempt it is those persons with "firm resolve" that interest us; it is those who "really intend," those whose purpose will be constant, and this no lie-detecting machine that tests one's mental state before action can reveal. The conduct in attempt is part of the meaning of the state we are concerned with detecting. In order to prevent harm, we believe it desirable to interfere with persons before they do all that they believe necessary to realize their intentions. This does not mean that we are punishing for mere intention. We are punishing such persons in the belief that they are members of the class of those who will not change their minds, the class of those whose purpose is constant. In interfering before the last step we must always feel some doubt that the person had the state that we label "firm resolve."

Second, suppose that the state could be defined independently of conduct and that machines could provide what the conduct is now taken to provide. There might still be good reason for distinguishing those persons who take substantial steps in furtherance of their intention from those who do not. First, the person who intends to assassinate a public official and who takes steps may be regarded as *making it* less likely that he will change his mind. The theory would be that the closer one gets to the actual commission of the deed the greater one's psychological commitment to perform the deed and the progressively diminishing probability of a change of mind and the corresponding progressively increased probability that harm will come about. One is, then, by one's acts putting oneself into a state that may be regarded as socially undesirable because it creates the risk that one will be less likely to change one's mind and this creates a greater risk that the harm we seek to prevent will come about. Further, the taking of steps makes it easier for the person to realize his aims. In this respect, too, it may be regarded as socially undesirable because in making it easier for harm to be done, it makes it more probable that harm will be done.

We can now turn to our second source of obscurity in the claim that "for law there must be external conduct."

II

When someone says "there must be external conduct" we may be troubled not just by what would and what would not be acceptable as external conduct but by the claim that there *must* be such conduct. How shall we take this claim? There are a number of possible interpretations.

First, when people thinking of law say "there must be external conduct," they may have in mind no more than what is and what is not in fact taken into account by all or most legal systems that have existed. They convey to us information that legal systems explicitly or implicitly preclude punishing persons for having or failing to have a certain state of mind. One who puts forward such a claim, if confronted by a case in which there is such an offense, may simply limit his generalization and admit that there are exceptions. Changes in the actual content of legal systems reflect on the adequacy of the claim and given a sufficiently large number of legal rules addressed to thought alone, one who makes such a claim may say, "it is no longer true that there must be external conduct." Such a reaction, of course, gives it away that the remark is not philosophical.

Second, it has been suggested that external conduct is necessary, for without outer signs it is impossible to prove inner states and were we not to insist upon some conduct we should have to rely upon unfounded charges. Blackstone wrote in explanation of the overt act requirement:

As no temporal tribunal can search the heart, or fathom the intentions of the mind, otherwise than as they are demonstrated by outward actions, it therefore cannot punish for what it cannot know. For which reason in all temporal jurisdictions an overt act, or some open evidence of an intended crime, is necessary in order to demonstrate the depravity of the will, before the man is liable to punishment.[16]

Blackstone appears to have believed that the overt requirement is justified by the limited access we have to the minds of others. This view differs from that of philosophers who have defended the view that "there must be external conduct" in at least two respects. First, there are situations in which by appropriate evidentiary requirements we might take into account our limited access to the minds of others and nevertheless be "punishing for thought alone." Second, were we to enact rules making certain mental states criminal and accept confessions as reliable evidence for conviction, Blackstone would not be troubled by the character of such enactments as laws. But it would be precisely their character as laws that would trouble the philosopher.

Third, someone may think that conduct is necessary in another way. The law, it might be argued, aims at promoting peace in the community. To this end there are rules that prohibit violence, theft, and deception and which set up institutions to interpret rules and to determine guilt. A legal system is a refined substitute, so it may be suggested, for private war. Now if we were to imagine a society in which all the rules were such that what people did to others was irrelevant for the applicability of the rules, then those rules could not possibly realize peace in the community. There must, then, be external conduct in precisely the same sense as a carpenter must use certain materials if he desires a chair to withstand pressure.[17]

First, it is not clear that such a system would totally fail to effectuate the aims of law. Suppose offenses were defined in terms of intentions to kill and in terms of those states of mind associated with reckless and negligent conduct. In principle many more persons would be guilty of legal wrongs within such a system than now are within our own. Those who intend to kill but who do not yet do anything would have committed a legal offense. But we might then accomplish what we now do and something besides. Those who now kill, steal, etc. would under this imagined system be punished as under our own. Their conduct would stand to their thoughts in precisely the relation that confessions stand to thoughts except that we might regard the conduct as more reliable evidence. When it was established that a person killed we should be able to infer the criminal state of mind. Thus, a failure to have the overt act requirement would not entirely defeat the aim of diminishing external harm. There are, however, two cautionary remarks needed here. Were the system to address itself to states of mind unrelated to harm, the system would presumably fail to effectuate these aims associated with law. And if all offenses consisted in the having of a state of mind and none in the doing of certain things, the system would be irrational in not rewarding restraint from harm. Persons who merely intend and those who do all that they believe necessary to realize their intentions would be treated alike. But, as we remarked above, this peculiarity, which we shall examine more carefully in a moment, does not mean that there would be a total lack of effectiveness to the system.

Suppose, however, that it were necessary to prohibit conduct in order to preserve peace in the community. The test of the philosophical character of the claim that "there must be external conduct" would be brought out in this way. If the system did not insist upon conduct for violation of the law, would this occasion the remark, "it's merely an ineffectual legal system," or the remark, "it's not a legal system at all or if it is, it is a very atypical one"? Is there an inclination to say that a legal rule prohibiting thought is not a legal rule or is there merely an inclination to say that it is impractical and ineffectual? The philosopher is inclined to make the former type of comment.

Fourth, in saying that "there must be external conduct," one may put forward a moral demand. The claim might be construed as "it is morally undesirable to make psychological states by themselves legally wrongful." The person who holds this view reacts to instances where thought is prohibited or required by law in this way: (1) he resembles the philosopher, for he doesn't withdraw his statement or claim, however many instances there are of legal rules that prohibit thought; (2) he differs from the philosopher because he isn't necessarily inclined to say such things as "it is not really law" or "it is a strange kind of law." He places a demand upon the content of legal rules which, if unsatisfied, reflects not on the enactment's being a law but on its being a moral law.

III

The claim that law insists upon external conduct may be unlike the claim that in fact legal systems do not punish for thought alone, unlike the claim that given our limited access to the minds of others legal systems must insist upon conduct, unlike the claim that in order to be effective legal systems must insist upon conduct, and unlike the claim that to be moral legal systems must insist upon a person's doing something wrong. What, then, is the character of the claim? It is, of course, a conceptual remark. Something is being said about the concept of law. We have now to look more closely at the character of the conceptual observation.

First, some philosophers believe that law is essentially linked to morality. For them a necessary condition for a rule to be a legal rule is that it not be immoral. Such philosophers may also believe that it is immoral to prohibit thought. They might, then, conclude that a rule making thought alone criminal was not a legal rule. They would reach this conclusion because they believe there exists some necessary connection between law and morality. This is one possible line of argument, but it has all the limitations associated with the view that an immoral law is not a law.

Second, a philosopher may believe that the connection between a legal rule and external conduct is more like the connection between being a legal rule and simply being a rule than it is like the connection between being a legal rule and being enforced by men rather than women. It is more like the connection between being a widow and being a woman than it is like the connection between being a woman and dying before one reaches the age of 120 years.

Such a philosopher may argue that it is not only more like the former types of cases than the latter but that it is precisely the same. He might recognize his divergence from ordinary usage by remarking about rules making thought alone criminal, "such rules aren't really legal rules." He would be aware that there is a difference between "if x is a legal rule, then x is a rule," and "if x is a legal rule, there must be external conduct." He is aware also that moral criticism of such enactments condemns them as "immoral laws."

Now what might account for the philosopher's straying from ordinary language? Let me suggest this possibility. He may be led to his position by an inability to find a comfortable middle-ground between "if x is a legal rule, then x is a rule" and "if x is a legal rule, then x is enforced by men." He compares the relation between a legal rule and external conduct with the relation between a legal rule and enforcement by men rather than women. He believes that were women to enforce the law it would not alter our judgment that it was law. But with respect to external conduct he feels the situation is different. Law seems to him an ordering for the promotion of peace and this seems to imply that regulating the conduct of people is connected with the meaning of law. When concepts are connected in meaning, it is natural to think them connected as a legal rule is connected with simply being rule, for that is so obviously a connection in meaning. But it seems clear that the concepts of legal rule and external conduct are not connected in that way. How, then, are they connected if they aren't connected as legal rules are connected with rules nor as enforcement by men is connected with legal rules?

Third, some may take this line. The connection is more subtle than that suggested by the philosopher who believes that a rule is not a legal rule unless it prohibits or requires conduct. Consider, again, the punishable offense of disbelieving in the story of creation. Is not such a rule a legal rule? There are several grounds for saying that it is. Such an enactment may resemble in a number of relevant particulars typical legal rules. And it may be an element in a system, the purpose of which is to promote values normally associated with law. Admitting this, someone might argue that law was still essentially a matter of preventing men from harming one another and that while this purpose is compatible with an atypical use of legal rules, it is not compatible with the general use of rules that prohibit merely thought. If we imagine a system, no rule of which is concerned with what men do but all of the rules of which are concerned exclusively with what they think, we would not be imagining a legal system. In saying, then, that "for law there must be external conduct" one may be making the point that it is necessarily the case for a system to be a legal system that some subset of its rules prohibit persons from harming one another. And this is like, someone might say, the connection between rules and a legal system, for while there are elements of legal systems that are not rules, it is necessary that there be at least some rules if there is to be a legal system at all.

This suggestion is bothersome. Suppose a system in which all of the rules defining offenses prohibit thought alone. Is such a system a legal system? The answer to this question is surely not as clear-cut as the answer to the question "Is a 'system' without rules a legal system?" We can surely foresee disputes arising over whether or not a system in which only thought is punished is a legal system. There is clearly something to be said in favor of the view that it is a legal system. It doesn't seem to me a necessary condition for a system to be a legal system that some, at least, of its rules prohibit persons from harming one another.

Fourth, it is possible, however, to claim that external conduct is connected in meaning with law and that it is not connected as the idea of a rule is connected with the idea of a legal system. It seems to me that the alternative I shall now elaborate provides the most defensible position.

Prohibiting harm stands to the idea of law as the legs of a chair stand to the idea of a chair. Neither the absence nor the presence of such a feature is determinative of a thing's being of a certain kind though it is relevant to a thing's being of a certain kind. That there are rules which prohibit harm is not a necessary condition for a system's being a legal system. That there are rules prohibiting harm is a feature that would incline one to classify a system as a legal system. That there are no rules prohibiting harm is relevant to classifying the system as other than a legal one. Prohibiting harm stands to the idea of law, I believe, as provision for a sanction stands to the idea of law. Not every legal rule need be supported by a sanction for the system of rules to be a legal system. But were a system of rules to have no provision whatsoever for sanctions, the general absence of the feature would weigh against our classifying the system as a legal one. Its absence is not, however, determinative of the system's being a legal system.

Now let us imagine two different types of system: (a) a system in which all of the rules prohibit or require states of mind believed to be unrelated to conduct that harms others, and (b) a system in which all the rules prohibit intentions to do harmful things and where our aim in making intentions criminal is to diminish harmful occurrences.

With respect to the first system there are apparent oddities and divergences from what would be regarded as a legal system. I want to elaborate on the second system, for the pull to say that it is a legal system seems to me stronger and if one appreciates the oddity of this system, a fortiori one will accept it with regard to the first system.

When we ask ourselves what is law or what is a legal system, a defining characteristic that naturally comes to mind is that of organized sanctions for the enforcement of rules. This feature has, of course, been regarded by some as an essential characteristic of law. Putting aside the issue of its essential character, it would be accepted, by most persons, as a feature quite central to our idea of law. The primary role of the sanction is to induce compliance among those who might be inclined to violate the rules. Sanctions, then, are provided for when there is law and these sanctions are, when the system is functioning, generally effective. If there were a system in which it was known that the sanctions provided for were never applied, we would only hesitantly, if at all, apply the label "legal" to the system.

Now if we turn to our imagined system in which all of the offenses are defined in terms of intentions to act, the following argument may be made. Threats of punishment in such a system play an entirely different role from what they do in most legal systems, for in law such threats generally operate to induce compliance with the rules among those inclined not to obey. In the system we have imagined, however, threats do not generally operate to induce compliance among those inclined to disobey. The threats operate merely to induce individuals to refrain from giving evidence of their criminal state. Thus, we would have a system in which the laws could, in general, be violated with impunity, a system, in other words, in which sanctions exist on paper but in which their characteristic role is absent. We have a system, then, that diverges in a respect relevant to classification from a clear case of a legal system.

I think that there is something wrong with this argument. With respect to some states of mind it has, I think, some validity. With respect to intentions I do not think that, as it stands, it is adequate.

Imagine the order, "Don't intend to raise your arm!" issued by one who has made it clear that if one does intend, the person will be shot. The foregoing line of argument would lead to the conclusion that this was an absurd type of situation. One could with impunity disobey the order, for the person ordered need only intend to raise his arm and not reveal his intention. We are to imagine a person who thinks to himself, "I'll intend to raise my arm but not raise my arm." But an order is not merely a form of words. In general, when one orders, one has the capacity to induce fear in a person that if he does not do what he is ordered to do he will suffer some harm. But here there is no such capacity nor would there generally be in such cases. Thus, one may conclude that it is not really an order or that it is an unusual kind of order.

There is, of course, something strange about this argument. If the person intends to raise his arm, this is no doubt compatible with his changing his mind and not raising his arm. But if one intends to raise one's arm, it is incompatible with one's believing that one will not raise one's arm where this belief derives from one's intending not to raise one's arm. In a word, if the person intends to raise his arm, he hasn't decided not to raise his arm. Thus, in ordering a person not to intend and threatening harm in case of disobedience, one may induce a person not to form an intention. From this it seems to follow that threats may play a role in a system in which one is prohibited from intending similar to the role they play in a system in which persons are prohibted from doing.

Still, there is something strange about ordering a person not to intend to raise his arm.[18] What is it? If one's aim is to induce a person not to intend to raise his arm, one can accomplish what one wishes by ordering him not to raise his arm. And if one's aim is to induce him not to raise his arm, the natural thing is to tell him not to. But more than this, if one were to order a person not to intend to raise his arm, one would be suggesting that one wanted him to refrain from doing something other than not raising his arm, that is, one would be suggesting that it was his intending that interested one and not his raising his arm. But if his raising his arm is what one wishes him not to do then simply ordering him not to raise his arm would accomplish what one wishes.

Nevertheless, there may be a point to framing laws, at least some laws, in terms of intentions rather than acts. There will be some persons who form intentions despite the existence of rules prohibiting the acts they intend to perform. By framing offenses in terms of intentions we may be enabled to interfere with such persons at the stage of intending and thus prevent them from doing what they intend to do. It is not, then, that a rule framed in terms of intentions has any greater deterrent value than one framed in terms of acts or harm but it may well have a greater preventive value. We have seen that this was so with respect to attempts.[19] We are to imagine, then, a system the thrust of which is primarily preventive rather than deterrent. Now, I think, that one can see that the implications of such a system are such that it diverges considerably from what we understand by a legal system.

First, the system we are considering is described as one whose aim is the prevention of harm. This emphasis on prevention of harm naturally inclines us toward regarding the system as a legal one, for this is a commonly accepted aim of legal systems. But given that this is the aim of our imagined system, what can account for its restricting its offenses to those that exclusively prohibit intentions? Mustn't a system with such an aim have some prohibitions on persons doing harm so as to encourage self-restraint at some point before commission of the harm that the law aims at preventing? Once the person reaches the stage at which he provides what the law regards as sufficient proof of intention he will have no incentive to restrain himself from continuing. With respect to this point, one may say that the system is irrational or that it is not as effective as it might be and yet argue that its irrationality does not reflect on whether or not it is a legal system.

Second, whatever truth there is in the view that there is an oddity in the idea of a legal system that exclusively prohibits thought must derive from our concept of law. What, then, are the features of this concept relevant to our inquiry?

Law is not merely a system of enforceable rules where the rules might have any content whatsoever.[20] The law establishes an ordering of men so as to reduce certain recognized evils. It involves an accommodation of the interests of human beings that may come into conflict. But there is more to it than this. The general, though not universal, rule is that violations of the law involve interferences with the interests of others. We can understand that there might be some laws—indeed all legal systems have such—whose violation did not occasion interference with others. But that laws might in general be violated and people remain unaffected conflicts with our concept of law. At the core of any legal system is a set of rules, then, general compliance with which provides benefits for all persons. The benefits consist in one's having a sphere of interests immune from interference by others. There is good reason for believing that one has a moral obligation to obey such rules. This obligation derives from the fairness of one's assuming certain burdens that others have assumed and which make these benefits possible. Further, it is reasonable to support such kinds of rules with sanctions, for if there were no sanctions for noncompliance, those who voluntarily complied with the rules would have no protection against those prepared to accept the benefits of the system without assuming the burdens. But the burdens one morally assumes are merely those which are necessary for persons to assume if the benefits of the system are in fact to accrue.

Now, the peculiarity of our imaginary system when compared with such law is that when the rules are violated the interests of others are unaffected. As long as persons restrain themselves from doing what they intend to do, interferences with others are avoided. It is never in the forming of an intention, the only thing made illegal, that one harms others. If the world were to change drastically we might harm others merely by forming intentions. But, then, of course, it would not be for mere intention that one was being punished. Under our imagined system, given men as we know them, harm can only come about from conduct. Still, general compliance with the rules prohibiting intention may be thought, like compliance with rules prohibiting conduct, to confer benefits of precisely the kind that a legal system normally confers and thus to impose upon all, as is the case when legal rules are involved, a moral obligation to obey such rules. No doubt, benefits would accrue if people did not form certain intentions. There would be a diminished risk of harm. But the benefits we associate with a legal system, namely the creation of a sphere of interests immune from interference, would also accrue if, given that persons formed intentions, they changed their minds and did not act in a way harmful to others. To be sure, in accepting the benefits of a system of rules one assumes the burdens necessary to realize those benefits. But one does not morally assume burdens beyond what is necessary. And because restraint from harming others is all that is necessary to achieve the aim of a sphere of interests immune from interference the only obligation derivable from acceptance of the benefits of such a system is not acting in certain ways. One doesn't, then, have an obligation to obey such "laws" as one has an obligation to obey laws that prohibit conduct. But, then, the system diverges from law as we understand it, for we commonly accept an obligation to obey the law.

Compare, too, the function of sanctions in our imagined system with their function in a legal system. Rules of law are such that those who voluntarily comply with them take on a special risk which becomes acceptable only because of the presence of sanctions which gives some assurance that those who voluntarily comply will not suffer at the hands of those who are not prepared to voluntarily comply.[21] But in a system in which exclusively intentions are prohibited, persons who do not form intentions that the system prohibits are not by such voluntary compliance with the rules, thereby putting themselves in any special way at the mercy of those who don't comply. Thus, the sanctions in such a system do not have their ordinary function, namely to reduce the risks of complying with the rules. Sufficient for protection of persons who voluntarily comply would be sanctions for persons acting in certain ways.

This paper opened with the claim "law is concerned with external conduct; morality with internal conduct." We had put aside any consideration of the claim with respect to morality. But have we, ironically, returned to issues of morality and come upon not some difference, but some connection between law and morality? It has been suggested, with some justification I believe, that it is a principle of a just constitution that "each person has the equal right to the most extensive liberty compatible with a like liberty for all."[22] Now if this is so, we can see that the system we have imagined involves a universal rejection of this principle. By merely intending to do harm one does not interfere with the liberty of others. Thus, in prohibiting intentions the law would deny a person a liberty compatible with a like liberty for all. But a system that did this as a general rule would also, I have argued, be a system that diverges from what we conceive of as a legal system. Is a system, then, that fails to give minimal respect to this principle of justice not only an unjust system but a system that diverges from what we understand as a legal system? I think so.

NOTES

1. E.g., law aims at a minimum; morality at a maximum. Law is prohibitive; morality is injunctive. The aim of law is not to punish sin but to prevent certain external results.
2. E.g., Edmond N. Cahn, *The Moral Decision* (Bloomington: Indiana University Press, 1955), pp. 44-46.
3. Rudolph Stammler, *Theory of Justice* (New York: Macmillan Co., 1925), p. 41.

4. Gustav Radbruch, "Legal Philosophy," *The Legal Philosophies of Lask, Radbruch and Dabin,* trans. K. Wilk (Cambridge, Mass.: Harvard University Press, 1950), p. 78.

5. Hermann Kantorowicz, *The Definition of Law* (Cambridge: Cambridge University Press, 1958), p. 43.

6. H. L. A. Hart, *The Concept of Law* (Oxford: Clarendon Press, 1961), p. 168.

7. I do not discuss in this essay those many difficult problems that arise if the states made punishable by law are ones over which we have no control.

8. *U.S. Constitution* Art. III Sec. 3: "No person shall be convicted of Treason unless on the Testimony of two Witnesses to the same overt Act, or on confession in open Court."

9. Supra, pp. 22-23.

10. See Glanville Williams, *Criminal Law* (London: Stevens & Sons, 1953), p. 485.

11. I do not wish to suggest by this that conduct is in no way connected with the meaning of intention. Certainly in some cases a person can intend to act without acting. Whether this could generally be the case and our concept of intention remain the same, I leave open.

12. Williams, *Criminal Law,* p. 485. In commenting on attempts: " . . . what of the supposed rule that repentance after the proximate act and before consummation of the full crime comes too late? Such repentance would seem to be the clearest indication that there was never a firm resolve whatever the accused himself may have thought."

13. See *State v. Grenz,* 26 Wash. 2d 764, 175 P. 2d 633, 637 (1946).

14. John Austin, *Lectures on Jurisprudence,* 5th ed. (London: John Murray, 1885), p. 441: "Where a criminal intention is evidenced by an attempt, the party is punished in respect of the criminal intention. . . . Why the party should be punished in respect of a mere intention, I will try to explain hereafter. The reason for requiring an attempt is probably the danger of admitting a mere confession. When coupled with an overt act, the confession is illustrated and supported by the latter. When not, it may proceed from insanity, or may be invented by the witness to it."

J. W. C. Turner, "Attempts to Commit Crimes," *Modern Approach to Criminal Law,* ed. Leon Radzinowicz and J. W. C. Turner (London: Macmillan Co., 1945), pp. 277-278: "The important point is, however, that the *actus reus* in attempt need not be forbidden in itself. It follows, therefore, that whereas in most crimes it is the *actus reus,* the harmful result, which the law desires to prevent, while the *mens rea* is only the necessary condition for the infliction of punishment on the person who produced the harmful result, in attempt the position is reversed, and it is the *mens rea* which the law regards as of primary importance and desires to prevent, while a sufficient *actus reus* is the necessary condition for the infliction of punishment on the person who formed the criminal intent. . . . If then, in attempt, the sole purpose of the *actus reus* is to establish the existence of *mens rea*, it is necessary to decide . . . what will be a sufficient *actus reus.*"

Patrick John Fitzgerald, *Criminal Law and Punishment* (Oxford: Clarendon Press, 1962), pp. 97-98: "An intention to commit a crime does not by itself suffice to make a person guilty of a crime. . . . Although mere criminal intention is not punishable, punishment is not reserved only for cases where the intention is fulfilled. Midway between the mere intention and the completed crime stands the inchoate crime of Attempt. . . . In some instances statutes provide a lesser punishment for the attempt than for the full offense. The reason is no doubt the fact that less harm results from the former than from the latter. In fact, here the law would seem to be penalizing mere criminal intention, contrary to the general rule."

Williams, *Criminal Law*, pp. 485-486: "Austin put forward the interesting view that in attempt the party is really punished for his intention, the act being required as evidence of a *firm* intention. There is much to be said for this. Admitting that intention in general can be proved by a confession, a confession is not sufficient proof in attempt because, standing alone, it gives no assurance that the accused would have had the constancy of purpose to put his plan into execution. The commission of the proximate act proves not merely the purpose but (in considerable degree) the firmness of the purpose."

Herbert Wechsler, William Kenneth Jones, and Harold L. Korn, "The Treatment of Inchoate Crimes in the Model Penal Code of the American Law Institute: Attempt, Solicitation, and Conspiracy," *Columbia Law Review* 61, no. 4 (1961), 573: ". . . the crime becomes essentially one of criminal purpose implemented by an overt act strongly corroborative of such purpose."

15. Cf. Wechsler, Jones, and Korn, "The Treatment of Inchoate Crimes," pp. 572-573.

16. William Blackstone, *Commentaries* Bk. IV, Chap. II.

17. Cf. Lon Fuller, *The Morality of Law* (New Haven: Yale University Press, 1964), p. 96. With respect to such features as the generality of legal rules, their promulgation, their clarity, etc., and the relation of such features to law he writes: "They are like the natural laws of carpentry, or at least those laws respected by a carpenter who wants the house he builds to remain standing and serve the purpose of those who live in it."

18. Cf. Austin, *Lectures on Jurisprudence*, pp. 460-461: "We might . . . be obliged to forbear from intentions, which respect future acts, or future forbearances from action; or, at least, to forbear from such of those intentions as are settled, deliberate, or frequently recurring to the mind. The fear of punishment might prevent the frequent recurrence; and might, therefore, prevent the pernicious acts or forbearances, to which intentions (when they recur frequently) certainly or probably lead."

19. Cf. Jerome Michael and Herbert Wechsler, "A Rationale of the Law of Homicide II," *Columbia Law Review* 37, no. 8 (1937), 1295-1296. Cf. also Wechsler, Jones, and Korn, "Treatment of Inchoate Crimes," p. 572:

"Since these offenses always presuppose a purpose to commit another crime, it is doubtful that the threat of punishment for their commission can significantly add to the deterrent efficacy of the sanction—which the actor by hypothesis ignores—that is threatened for the crime that is his object. There may be cases where this may occur, as when the actor thinks the chance of apprehension low if he succeeds but high if he should fail in his attempt, or when reflection that otherwise would be postponed until too late is promoted at an early stage—which may be true of some conspiracies. These are, however, special situations. Viewed generally, it seems clear that deterrence is at most a minor function to be served in fashioning provisions of the penal law addressed to inchoate crimes; that burden is discharged by the law dealing with the substantive offenses."

20. That the legal rules regulate conduct and not thought is usually assumed. One need only recall classic definitions of law.

21. Cf. Hart, *The Concept of Law*, p. 193.

22. John Rawls put forward this claim in "Justice as Fairness," *Philosophical Review* 67 (1958), 164.

2 Persons and Punishment

They acted and looked . . . at us, and around in our house, in a way that had about it the feeling— at least for me—that we were not people. In their eyesight we were just things, that was all.
                                                                          Malcolm X
We have no right to treat a man like a dog.
                                                        Governor Lester Maddox

ALFREDO Traps in Durrenmatt's tale discovers that he has brought off, all by himself, a murder involving considerable ingenuity. The mock prosecutor in the tale demands the death penalty "as reward for a crime that merits admiration, astonishment, and respect." Traps is deeply moved; indeed, he is exhilarated, and the whole of his life becomes more heroic, and, ironically, more precious. His defense attorney proceeds to argue that Traps was not only innocent but incapable of guilt, "a victim of the age." This defense Traps disavows with indignation and anger. He makes claim to the murder as his and demands the prescribed punishment—death.

The themes to be found in this macabre tale do not often find their way into philosophical discussions of punishment. These discussions deal with large and significant questions of whether or not we ever have the right to punish, and if we do, under what

Reprinted from *The Monist* (October 1968).

31

conditions, to what degree, and in what manner. There is a tradition, of course, not notable for its present vitality, that is closely linked with motifs in Durrenmatt's tale of crime and punishment. Its adherents have urged that justice requires a person be punished if he is guilty. Sometimes—though rarely—these philosophers have expressed themselves in terms of the criminal's *right to be punished*. Reaction to the claim that there is such a right has been astonishment combined, perhaps, with a touch of contempt for the perversity of the suggestion. A strange right that no one would ever wish to claim! With that flourish the subject is buried and the right disposed of. In this paper the subject is resurrected.

My aim is to argue for four propositions concerning rights that will certainly strike some as not only false but preposterous: first, that we have a right to punishment; second, that this right derives from a fundamental human right to be treated as a person; third, that this fundamental right is a natural, inalienable, and absolute right; and, fourth, that the denial of this right implies the denial of all moral rights and duties. Showing the truth of one, let alone all, of these large and questionable claims, is a tall order. The attempt or, more properly speaking, the first steps in an attempt, follow.

1. When someone claims that there is a right to be free, we can easily imagine situations in which the right is infringed and easily imagine situations in which there is a point to asserting or claiming the right. With the right to be punished, matters are otherwise. The immediate reaction to the claim that there is such a right is puzzlement. And the reasons for this are apparent. People do not normally value pain and suffering. Punishment is associated with pain and suffering. When we think about punishment we naturally think of the strong desire most persons have to avoid it, to accept, for example, acquittal of a criminal charge with relief and eagerly, if convicted, to hope for pardon or probation. Adding, of course, to the paradoxical character of the claim of such a right is difficulty in imagining circumstances in which it would be denied one. When would one rightly demand punishment and meet with any threat of the claim being denied?

So our first task it to see when the claim of such a right would have a point. I want to approach this task by setting out two complex types of institutions both of which are designed to maintain some degree of social control. In the one a central concept is punishment for wrongdoing and in the other the central concepts are control of dangerous individuals and treatment of disease.

Let us first turn attention to the institutions in which punishment is involved. The institutions I describe will resemble those we ordinarily think of as institutions of punishment; they will have, however, additional features we associate with a system of just punishment.

Let us suppose that men are constituted roughly as they now are, with a rough equivalence in strength and abilities, a capacity to be injured by each other and to make judgments that such injury is undesirable, a limited strength of will, and a capacity to reason and to conform conduct to rules. Applying to the conduct of these men are a group of rules, ones I shall label "primary," which closely resemble the core rules of our criminal law, rules that prohibit violence and deception and compliance with which provides benefits for all persons. These benefits consist of noninterference by others with what each person values, such matters as continuance of life and bodily security. The rules define a sphere for each person then, which is immune from interference by others. Making possible this mutual benefit is the assumption by individuals of a burden. The burden consists in the exercise of self-restraint by individuals over inclinations that would, if satisfied, directly interfere or create a substantial risk of interference with others in proscribed ways. If a person fails to exercise self-restraint even though he might have and gives in to such inclinations, he renounces a burden which others have voluntarily assumed and thus gains an advantage which others, who have restrained themselves, do not possess. This system, then, is one in which the rules establish a mutuality of benefit and burden and in which the benefits of noninterference are conditional upon the assumption of burdens.

Connecting punishment with the violation of these primary rules, and making public the provision for punishment, is both reasonable and just. First, it is only reasonable that those who voluntarily comply with the rules be provided some assurance that they will not be assuming burdens which others are unprepared to assume. Their disposition to comply voluntarily will diminish as they learn that others are with impunity renouncing burdens they are assuming. Second, fairness dictates that a system in which benefits and burdens are equally distributed have a mechanism designed to prevent a maldistribution in the benefits and burdens. Thus, sanctions are attached to noncompliance with the primary rules so as to induce compliance with the primary rules among those who may be disinclined to obey. In this way the likelihood of an unfair distribution is diminished.

Third, it is just to punish those who have violated the rules and caused the unfair distribution of benefits and burdens. A person who violates the rules has something others have—the benefits of the system—but by renouncing what others have assumed, the burdens of self-restraint, he has acquired an unfair advantage. Matters are not even until this advantage is in some way erased. Another way of putting it is that he owes something to others, for he has something that does not rightfully belong to him. Justice—that is punishing such individuals—restores the equilibrium of benefits and burdens by taking from the individual what he owes, that is, exacting the debt. It is important to see that the equilibrium may be restored in another way. Forgiveness—with its legal analogue of a pardon—while not the righting of an unfair distribution by making one pay his debt is, nevertheless, a restoring of the equilibrium by forgiving the debt. Forgiveness may be viewed, at least in some types of cases, as a gift after the fact, erasing a debt, which had the gift been given before the fact, would not have created a debt. But the practice of pardoning has to proceed sensitively, for it may endanger in a way the practice of justice does not, the maintenance of an equilibrium of benefits and burdens. If all are indiscriminately pardoned less incentive is provided individuals to restrain their inclinations, thus increasing the incidence of persons taking what they do not deserve.

There are also in this system we are considering a variety of operative principles compliance with which provides some guarantee that the system of punishment does not itself promote an unfair distribution of benefits and burdens. For one thing, provision is made for a variety of defenses, each one of which can be said to have as its object diminishing the chances of forcibly depriving a person of benefits others have if that person has not derived an unfair advantage. A person has not derived an unfair advantage if he could not have restrained himself or if it is unreasonable to expect him to behave otherwise than he did. Sometimes the rules preclude punishment of classes of persons such as children. Sometimes they provide a defense if on a particular occasion a person lacked the capacity to conform his conduct to the rules. Thus, someone who in an epileptic seizure strikes another is excused. Punishment in these cases would be punishment of the innocent, punishment of those who do not voluntarily renounce a burden others have assumed. Punishment in such cases, then, would not equalize but rather cause an unfair distribution in benefits and burdens.

Along with principles providing defenses there are requirements that the rules be prospective and relatively clear so that persons have a fair opportunity to comply with the rules. There are, also, rules governing, among other matters, the burden of proof, who shall bear it and what it shall be, the prohibition on double jeopardy, and the privilege against self-incrimination. Justice requires conviction of the guilty, and requires their punishment, but in setting out to fulfill the demands of justice we may, of course, because we are not omniscient, cause injustice by convicting and punishing the innocent. The resolution arrived at in the system I am describing consists in weighing as the greater evil the punishment of the innocent. The primary function of the system of rules was to provide individuals with a sphere of interest immune from interference. Given this goal, it is determined to be a greater evil for society to interfere unjustifiably with an individual by depriving him of good than for the society to fail to punish those that have unjustifiably interfered.

Finally, because the primary rules are designed to benefit all and because the punishments prescribed for their violation are publicized and the defenses respected, there is some plausibility in the exaggerated claim that in choosing to do an act violative of the rules an individual has chosen to be punished. This way of putting matters brings to our attention the extent to which, when the system is as I have described it, the criminal "has brought the punishment upon himself" in contrast to those cases where it would be misleading to say "he has brought in upon himself," cases, for example, where one does not know the rules or is punished in the absence of fault.

To summarize, then: first, there is a group of rules guiding the behavior of individuals in the community which establish spheres of interest immune from interference by others; second, provision is made for what is generally regarded as a deprivation of some thing of value if the rules are violated; third, the deprivations visited upon any person are justified by that person's having violated the rules; fourth, the deprivation, in this just system of punishment, is linked to rules that fairly distribute benefits and burdens and to procedures that strike some balance between not punishing the guilty and punishing the innocent, a class defined as those who have not voluntarily done acts violative of the law, in which it is evident that the evil of punishing the innocent is regarded as greater than the nonpunishment of the guilty.

At the core of many actual legal systems one finds, of course, rules and procedures of the kind I have sketched. It is obvious, though, that any ongoing legal system differs in significant respects from what I have presented here, containing "pockets of injustice."

I want now to sketch an extreme version of a set of institutions of a fundamentally different kind, institutions proceeding on a conception of man which appears to be basically at odds with that operative within a system of punishment.

Rules are promulgated in this system that prohibit certain types of injuries and harms.

In this world we are now to imagine when an individual harms another his conduct is to be regarded as a symptom of some pathological condition in the way a running nose is a symptom of a cold. Actions diverging from some conception of the normal are viewed as manifestations of a disease in the way in which we might today regard the arm and leg movements of an epileptic during a seizure. Actions conforming to what is normal are assimilated to the normal and healthy functioning of bodily organs. What a person does, then, is assimilated, on this conception, to what we believe today, or at least most of us believe today, a person undergoes. We draw a distinction between the operation of the kidney and raising an arm on request. This distinction between mere events or happenings and human actions is erased in our imagined system.[1]

There is, however, bound to be something strange in this erasing of a recognized distinction, for, as with metaphysical suggestions generally, and I take this to be one, the distinction may be reintroduced but given a different description, for example, "happenings with X type of causes" and "happenings with Y type of causes." Responses of different kinds, today legitimated by our distinction between happenings and actions may be legitimated by this new manner of description. And so there may be isomorphism between a system recognizing the distinction and one erasing it. Still, when this distinction is erased certain tendencies of thought and responses might naturally arise that would tend to affect unfavorably values respected by a system of punishment.

Let us elaborate on this assimilation of conduct of a certain kind to symptoms of a disease. First, there is something abnormal in both the case of conduct, such as killing another, and a symptom of a disease such as an irregular heart beat. Second, there are causes for this abnormality in action such that once we know of them we can explain the abnormality as we now can explain the symptoms of many physical diseases. The abnormality is looked upon as a happening with a causal explanation rather than an action for which there were reasons. Third, the causes that account for the abnormality interfere with the normal functioning of the body, or, in the case of killing with what is regarded as a normal functioning of an individual. Fourth, the abnormality is in some way a part of the individual, necessarily involving his body. A well going dry might satisfy our three foregoing conditions of disease symptoms, but it is hardly a disease or the symptom of one. Finally, and most obscure, the abnormality arises in some way from within the individual. If Jones is hit with a mallet by Smith, Jones may reel about and fall on James who may be injured. But this abnormal conduct of Jones is not regarded as a symptom of disease. Smith, not Jones, is suffering from some pathological condition.

With this view of man the institutions of social control respond, not with punishment, but with either preventive detention, in case of "carriers," or therapy in the case of those manifesting pathological symptoms. The logic of sickness implies the logic of therapy. And therapy and punishment differ widely in their implications. In bringing out some of these differences I want again to draw attention to the important fact that while the distinctions we now draw are erased in the therapy world, they may, in fact, be reintroduced but under different descriptions. To the extent they are, we really have a punishment system combined with a therapy system. I am concerned now, however, with what the implications would be were the world indeed one of therapy and not a disguised world of punishment and therapy, for I want to suggest tendencies of thought that arise when one is immersed in the ideology of disease and therapy.

First, punishment is the imposition upon a person who is believed to be at fault of something commonly believed to be a deprivation where that deprivation is justified by the person's guilty behavior. It is associated with resentment, for the guilty are those who have done what they had no right to do by failing to exercise restraint when they might have and where others have. Therapy is not a response to a person who is at fault. We respond to an individual, not because of what he has done, but because of some condition from which he is suffering. If he is no longer suffering from the condition, treatment no longer has a point. Punishment, then, focuses on the past; therapy on the present. Therapy is normally associated with compassion for what one undergoes, not resentment for what one has illegitimately done.

Second, with therapy, unlike punishment, we do not seek to deprive the person of something acknowledged as a good, but seek rather to help and to benefit the individual who is suffering by ministering to his illness in the hope that the person can be cured.

The good we attempt to do is not a reward for desert. The individual suffering has not merited by his disease the good we seek to bestow upon him but has, because he is a creature that has the capacity to feel pain, a claim upon our sympathies and help.

Third, we saw with punishment that its justification was related to maintaining and restoring a fair distribution of benefits and burdens. Infliction of the prescribed punishment carries the implication, then, that one has "paid one's debt" to society, for the punishment is the taking from the person of something commonly recognized as valuable. It is this conception of "a debt owed" that may permit, as I suggested earlier, under certain conditions, the nonpunishment of the guilty, for operative within a system of punishment may be a concept analogous to forgiveness, namely pardoning. Who it is that we may pardon and under what conditions—contrition with its elements of self-punishment no doubt plays a role—I shall not go into though it is clearly a matter of the greatest practical and theoretical interest. What is clear is that the conceptions of "paying a debt" or "having a debt forgiven" or pardoning have no place in a system of therapy.

Fourth, with punishment there is an attempt at some equivalence between the advantage gained by the wrongdoer—partly based upon the seriousness of the interest invaded, partly on the state of mind with which the wrongful act was performed—and the punishment meted out. Thus, we can understand a prohibition on "cruel and unusual punishments" so that disproportionate pain and suffering are avoided. With therapy attempts at proportionality make no sense. It is perfectly plausible giving someone who kills a pill and treating for a lifetime within an institution one who has broken a dish and manifested accident proneness. We have the concept of "painful treatment." We do not have the concept of "cruel treatment." Because treatment is regarded as a benefit, though it may involve pain, it is natural that less restraint is exercised in bestowing it, than in inflicting punishment. Further, protests with respect to treatment are likely to be assimilated to the complaints of one whose leg must be amputated in order for him to live, and, thus, largely disregarded. To be sure, there is operative in the therapy world some conception of the "cure being worse than the disease," but if the disease is manifested in conduct harmful to others, and if being a normal operating human being is valued highly, there will naturally be considerable pressure to find the cure acceptable.

Fifth, the rules in our system of punishment governing conduct of individuals were rules violation of which involved either direct interference with others or the creation of a substantial risk of such interference. One could imagine adding to this system of primary rules other rules proscribing preparation to do acts violative of the primary rules and even rules proscribing thoughts. Objection to such suggestions would have many sources but a principal one would consist in its involving the infliction of punishment on too great a number of persons who would not, because of a change of mind, have violated the primary rules. Though we are interested in diminishing violations of the primary rules, we are not prepared to punish too many individuals who would never have violated the rules in order to achieve this aim. In a system motivated solely by a preventive and curative ideology there would be less reason to wait until symptoms manifest themselves in socially harmful conduct. It is understandable that we should wish at the earliest possible stage to arrest the development of the disease. In the punishment system, because we are dealing with deprivations, it is understandable that we should forbear from imposing them until we are quite sure of guilt. In the therapy system, dealing as it does with benefits, there is less reason for forbearance from treatment at an early stage.

Sixth, a variety of procedural safeguards we associate with punishment have less significance in a therapy system. To the degree objections to double jeopardy and self-incrimination are based on a wish to decrease the chances of the innocent being convicted and punished, a therapy system, unconcerned with this problem, would disregard such safeguards. When one is out to help people there is also little sense in urging that the burden of proof be on those providing the help. And there is less point to imposing the burden of proving that the conduct was pathological beyond a reasonable doubt. Further, a jury system which, within a system of justice, serves to make accommodations to the individual situation and to introduce a human element, would play no role or a minor one in a world where expertise is required in making determinations of disease and treatment.

In our system of punishment an attempt was made to maximize each individual's freedom of choice by first of all delimiting by rules certain spheres of conduct immune from interference by others. The punishment associated with these primary rules paid deference to an individual's free choice by connecting punishment to a freely chosen act violative of the rules, thus giving some plausibility to the claim, as we saw, that what a person received by way of punishment he himself had chosen. With the world of disease and therapy all this changes and the individual's free choice ceases to be a determinative factor in how others respond to him. All those principles of our own legal system that minimize the chances of punishment of those who have not chosen to do acts violative of the rules tend to lose their point in the therapy system, for how we respond in a therapy system to a person is not conditioned upon what he has chosen but rather on what symptoms he has manifested or may manifest and what the best therapy for the disease is that is suggested by the symptoms.

Now, it is clear, I think, that were we confronted with the alternatives I have sketched, between a system of just punishment and a thoroughgoing system of treatment, a system, that is, that did not reintroduce concepts appropriate to punishment, we could see the point in claiming that a person has a right to be punished, meaning by this that a person had a right to all those institutions and practices linked to punishment. For these would provide him with, among other things, a far greater ability to predict what would happen to him on the occurrence of certain events than the therapy system. There is the inestimable value to each of us of having the responses of others to us determined over a wide range of our lives by what we choose rather than what they choose. A person has a right to institutions that respect his choices. Our punishment system does; our therapy system does not.

Apart from those aspects of our therapy model which would

relate to serious limitations on personal liberty, there are clearly objections of a more profound kind to the mode of thinking I have associated with the therapy model.

First, human beings pride themselves in having capacities that animals do not. A common way, for example, of arousing shame in a child is to compare the child's conduct to that of an animal. In a system where all actions are assimilated to happenings we are assimilated to creatures—indeed, it is more extreme than this— whom we have always thought possessed of less than we. Fundamental to our practice of praise and order of attainment is that one who can do more—one who is capable of more and one who does more is more worthy of respect and admiration. And we have thought of ourselves as capable where animals are not of making, of creating, among other things, ourselves. The conception of man I have outlined would provide us with a status that today, when our conduct is assimilated to it in moral criticism, we consider properly evocative of shame.

Second, if all human conduct is viewed as something men undergo, thrown into question would be the appropriateness of that extensive range of peculiarly human satisfactions that derive from a sense of achievement. For these satisfactions we shall have to substitute those mild satisfactions attendant upon a healthy well-functioning body. Contentment is our lot if we are fortunate; intense satisfaction at achievement is entirely inappropriate.

Third, in the therapy world nothing is earned and what we receive comes to us through compassion, or through a desire to control us. Resentment is out of place. We can take credit for nothing but must always regard ourselves—if there are selves left to regard once actions disappear—as fortunate recipients of benefits or unfortunate carriers of disease who must be controlled. We know that within our own world human beings who have been so regarded and who come to accept this view of themselves come to look upon themselves as worthless. When what we do is met with resentment, we are indirectly paid something of a compliment.

Fourth, attention should also be drawn to a peculiar evil that may be attendant upon regarding a man's actions as symptoms of disease. The logic of cure will push us toward forms of therapy that inevitably involve changes in the person made against his will. The evil in this would be most apparent in those cases where the agent, whose action is determined to be a manifestation of some disease, does not regard his action in this way. He believes that what he has done is, in fact, "right" but his conception of "normality" is not the therapeutically accepted one. When we treat an illness we normally treat a condition that the person is not responsible for. He is "suffering" from some disease and we treat the condition, relieving the person of something preventing his normal functioning. When we begin treating persons for actions that have been chosen, we do not lift from the person something that is interfering with his normal functioning but we change the person so that he functions in a way regarded as normal by the current therapeutic community. We have to change him and his judgments of value. In doing this we display a lack of respect for the moral status of individuals, that is, a lack of respect for the reasoning and choices of individuals. They are but animals who must be conditioned. I think we can understand and, indeed, sympathize with a man's preferring death to being forcibly turned into what he is not.

Finally, perhaps most frightening of all would be the derogation in status of all protests to treatment. If someone believes that he has done something right, and if he protests being treated and changed, the protest will itself be regarded as a sign of some pathological condition, for who would not wish to be cured of an affliction? What this leads to are questions of an important kind about the effect of this conception of man upon what we now understand by reasoning. Here what a person takes to be a reasoned defense of an act is treated, as the action was, on the model of a happening of a pathological kind. Not just a person's acts are taken from him but also his attempt at a reasoned justification for the acts. In a system of punishment a person who has committed a crime may argue that what he did was right. We make him pay the price and we respect his right to retain the judgment he has made. A conception of pathology precludes this form of respect.

It might be objected to the foregoing that all I have shown—if that—is that if the only alternatives open to us are a *just* system of punishment or the mad world of being treated like sick or healthy animals, we do in fact have a right to a system of punishment of this kind. But this hardly shows that we have a right *simpliciter* to punishment as we do, say, to be free. Indeed, it does not even show a right to a just system of punishment, for surely we can, without too much difficulty, imagine situations in which the alternatives to punishment are not this mad world but a world in which we are still treated as persons and there is, for example, not the pain and suffering attendant upon punishment. One such world is one in which there are rules but responses to their violation is not the deprivation of some good but forgiveness. Still another type of world would be one in which violation of the rules were responded to by merely comparing the conduct of the person to something commonly regarded as low or filthy, and thus, producing by this mode of moral criticism, feelings of shame rather than feelings of guilt.

I am prepared to allow that these objections have a point. While granting force to the above objections I want to offer a few additional comments with respect to each of them. First, any existent legal system permits the punishment of individuals under circumstances where the conditions I have set forth for a just system have not been satisfied. A glaring example of this would be criminal strict liability which is to be found in our own legal system. Nevertheless, I think it would be difficult to present any system we should regard as a system of punishment that would not still have a great advantage over our imagined therapy system. The system of punishment we imagine may more and more approximate a system of sheer terror in which human beings are treated as animals to be intimidated and prodded. To the degree that the system is of this character it is, in my judgment, not simply an unjust system but one that diverges from what we normally understand by a system of punishment. At least some deference to the choice of individuals is built into the idea of punishment. So there would be some truth in saying we have a right to any system of punishment if the only alternative to it was therapy.

Second, people may imagine systems in which there are rules and in which the response to their violation is not punishment but pardoning, the legal analogue of forgiveness. Surely this is a system to which we would claim a right as against one in which we are made to suffer for violating the rules. There are several comments that need to be made about this. It may be, of course, that a high incidence of pardoning would increase the incidence of rule violations. Further, the difficulty with suggesting pardoning as a general response is that pardoning presupposes the very responses that it is suggested it supplant. A system of deprivations, or a practice of deprivations on the happening of certain actions, underlies the practice of pardoning and forgiving, for it is only where we possess the idea of wrong to be made up or of a debt owed to others, ideas we acquire within a world in which there have been deprivations for wrong acts, that we have the idea of pardoning for the wrong or forgiving the debt.

Finally, if we look at the responses I suggested would give rise to feelings of shame, we may rightly be troubled with the appropriateness of this response in any community in which each person assumes burdens so that each may derive benefits. In such situations might it not be that individuals have a right to a system of punishment so that each person could be assured that inequities in the distribution of benefits and burdens are unlikely to occur and if they do, procedures exist for correcting them? Further, it may well be that, everything considered, we should prefer the pain and suffering of a system of punishment to a world in which we only experience shame on the doing of wrong acts, for with guilt there are relatively simple ways of ridding ourselves of the feeling we have, that is gaining forgiveness or taking the punishment, but with shame we have to bear it until we no longer are the person who has behaved in the shameful way. Thus, I suggest that we have, wherever there is a distribution of benefits and burdens of the kind I have described, a right to a system of punishment.

I want also to make clear in concluding this section that I have argued, though very indirectly, not just for a right to a system of punishment, but for a right to be punished once there is in existence such a system. Thus, a man has the right to be punished rather than treated if he is guilty of some offense. And, indeed, one can imagine a case in which, even in the face of an offer of a pardon, a man claims and ought to have acknowledged his right to be punished.

2. The primary reason for preferring the system of punishment as against the system of therapy might have been expressed in terms of the one system treating one as a person and the other not. In invoking the right to be punished, one justifies one's claim by reference to a more fundamental right. I want now to turn attention to this fundamental right and attempt to shed light—it will have to be little, for the topic is immense—on what is meant by "treating an individual as a person."

When we talk of not treating a human being as a person or "showing no respect for one as a person" what we imply by our words is a contrast between the manner in which one acceptably responds to human beings and the manner in which one acceptably responds to animals and inanimate objects. When we treat a human being merely as an animal or some inanimate object our responses to the human being are determined, not by his choices, but ours in disregard of or with indifference to his. And when we "look upon" a person as less than a person or not a person, we consider the person as incapable of rational choice. In cases of not treating a human being as a person we interfere with a person in such a way that what is done, even if the person is involved in the doing, is done not by the person but by the user of the person. In extreme cases there may even be an elision of a causal chain so that we might say that X killed Z even though Y's hand was the hand that held the weapon, for Y's hand may have been entirely in X's control. The one agent is in some way treating the other as a mere link in a causal chain. There is, of course, a wide range of cases in which a person is used to accomplish the aim of another and in which the person used is less than fully free. A person may be grabbed against his will and used as a shield. A person may be drugged or hypnotized and then employed for certain ends. A person may be deceived into doing other than he intends doing. A person may be ordered to do something and threatened with harm if he does not and coerced into doing what he does not want to. There is still another range of cases in which individuals are not used, but in which decisions by others are made that affect them in circumstances where they have the capacity for choice and where they are not being treated as persons.

But it is particularly important to look at coercion, for I have claimed that a just system of punishment treats human beings as persons; and it is not immediately apparent how ordering someone to do something and threatening harm differs essentially from having rules supported by threats of harm in case of non-compliance.

There are affinities between coercion and other cases of not treating someone as a person, for it is not the coerced person's choices but the coercer's that are responsible for what is done. But unlike other indisputable cases of not treating one as a person, for example using someone as a shield, there is some choice involved in coercion. And if this is so, why does the coercer stand in any different relation to the coerced person than the criminal law stands to individuals in society?

Suppose the person who is threatened disregards the order and gets the threatened harm. Now suppose he is told, "Well, you did after all bring it upon yourself." There is clearly something strange in this. It is the person doing the threatening and not the person threatened who is responsible. But our reaction to punishment, at least in a system that resembles the one I have described, is precisely that the person violating the rules brought it upon himself. What lies behind these different reactions?

There exist situations in the law, of course, which resemble coercion situations. There are occasions when in the law a person might justifiably say "I am not being treated as a person but being used" and where he might properly react to the punishment as something "he was hardly responsible for." But it is possible to have a system in which it would be misleading to say, over a wide range of cases of punishment for noncompliance, that we are using persons. The clearest case in which it would be inappropriate to so regard punishment would be one in which there were explicit agreements in advance that punishment should follow on the voluntary doing of certain acts. Even if one does not have such conditions satisfied, and obviously such explicit agreements are not characteristic, one can see significant differences between our system of just punishment and a coercion situation.

First, unlike the case with one person coercing another "to do his will," the rules in our system apply to all, with the benefits and burdens equally distributed. About such a system it cannot be said that some are being subordinated to others or are being used by others or gotten to do things by others. To the extent that the rules are thought to be to the advantage of only some or to the extent there is a maldistribution of benefits and burdens, the difference between coercion and law disappears.

Second, it might be argued that at least any person inclined to act in a manner violative of the rules stands to all others as the person coerced stands to his coercer, and that he, at least, is a person disadvantaged as others are not. It is important here, I think, that he is part of a system in which it is commonly agreed that forbearance from the acts proscribed by the rules provides advantages for all. This system is the accepted setting; it is the norm. Thus, in any coercive situation, it is the coercer who deviates from the norm, with the responsibility of the person he is attempting to coerce, defeated. In a just punishment situation, it is the person deviating from the norm, indeed he might be a coercer, who is responsible, for it is the norm to restrain oneself from acts of that kind. A voluntary agent diverging in his conduct from what is expected or what the norm is, on general causal principles, regarded as the cause of what results from his conduct.

There is, then, some plausibility in the claim that, in a system of punishment of the kind I have sketched, a person chooses the punishment that is meted out to him. If, then, we can say in such a system that the rules provide none with advantages that others do not have, and further, that what happens to a person is conditioned by that person's choice and not that of others, then we can say that it is a system responding to one as a person.

We treat a human being as a person provided, first, we permit the person to make the choices that will determine what happens to him and, second, when our responses to the person are responses respecting the person's choices. When we respond to a person's illness by treating the illness it is neither a case of treating or not treating the individual as a person. When we give a person a gift we are neither treating or not treating him as a person, unless, of course, he does not wish it, chooses not to have it, but we compel him to accept it.

3. This right to be treated as a person is a fundamental human right belonging to all human beings by virtue of their being human. It is also a natural, inalienable, and absolute right. I want now to defend these claims so reminiscent of an era of philosophical thinking about rights that many consider to have been seriously confused.

If the right is one that we possess by virtue of being human beings, we are immediately confronted with an apparent dilemma. If, to treat another as a person requires that we provide him with reasons for acting and avoid force or deception, how can we justify the force and deception we exercise with respect to children and the mentally ill? If they, too, have a right to be treated as persons are we not constantly infringing their rights? One way out of this is simply to restrict the right to those who satisfy the conditions of being a person. Infants and the insane, it might be argued, do not meet these conditions, and they would not then have the right. Another approach would be to describe the right they possess as a prima facie right to be treated as a person. This right might then be outweighed by other considerations. This approach generally seems to me, as I shall later argue, inadequate.

I prefer this tack. Children possess the right to be treated as persons but they possess this right as an individual might be said in the law of property to possess a future interest. There are advantages in talking of individuals as having a right though complete enjoyment of it is postponed. Brought to our attention, if we ascribe to them the right, is the legitimacy of their complaint if they are not provided with opportunities and conditions assuring their full enjoyment of the right when they acquire the characteristics of persons. More than this, all persons are charged with the sensitive task of not denying them the right to be a person and to be treated as a person by failing to provide the conditions for their becoming individuals who are able freely and in an informed way to choose and who are prepared themselves to assume responsibility for their choices. There is an obligation imposed upon us all, unlike that we have with respect to animals, to respond to children in such a way as to maximize the chances of their becoming persons. This may well impose upon us the obligation to treat them as persons from a very early age, that is, to respect their choices and to place upon them the responsibility for the choices to be made. There is no need to say that there is a close connection between how we respond to them and what they become. It also imposes upon us all the duty to display constantly the qualities of a person, for what they become they will largely become because of what they learn from us is acceptable behavior.

In claiming that the right is a right that human beings have by virtue of being human, there are several other features of the right that should be noted, perhaps better conveyed by labelling them "natural." First, it is a right we have apart from any voluntary agreement into which we have entered. Second, it is not a right that derives from some defined position or status. Third, it is equally apparent that one has the right regardless of the society or community of which one is a member. Finally, it is a right linked to certain features of a class of beings. Were we fundamentally different than we now are, we would not have it. But it is more than that, for the right is linked to a feature of human beings which were that feature absent—the capacity to reason and to choose on the basis of reasons—profound conceptual changes would be involved in the thought about human beings. It is a right, then, connected with a feature of men that sets men apart from other natural phenomena.

The right to be treated as a person is inalienable. To say of a right that it is inalienable draws attention not to limitations placed on what others may do with respect to the possessor of the right but rather to limitations placed on the dispositive capacities of the possessor of the right. Something is to be gained in keeping the issues of alienability and absoluteness separate.

There are a variety of locutions qualifying what possessors of rights may and may not do. For example, on this issue of alienability, it would be worthwhile to look at, among other things, what is involved in abandoning, abdicating, conveying, giving up, granting, relinquishing, surrendering, transferring, and waiving one's rights. And with respect to each of these concepts we should also have to be sensitive to the variety of uses of the term "rights." What it is, for example, to waive a Hohfeldian "right" in his strict sense will differ from what it is to waive a right in his "privilege" sense.

Let us look at only two concepts very briefly, those of transferring and waiving rights. The clearest case of transferring rights is that of transferring rights with respect to specific objects. I own a watch and owning it I have a complicated relationship, captured in this area rather well I think by Hohfeld's four basic legal relationships, to all persons in the world with respect to the watch. We crudely capture these complex relationships by talking of my "property rights" in or with respect to the watch. If I sell the watch, thus exercising a capacity provided by the rules of property, I have transferred rights in or with respect to the watch to someone else, the buyer, and the buyer now stands, as I formerly did, to all persons in the world in a series of complex relationships with respect to the watch.

While still the owner, I may have given to another permission to use it for several days. Had there not been the permission and had the person taken the watch, we should have spoken of interfering with or violating or, possibly, infringing my property rights. Or, to take a situation in which tranferring rights is inappropriate, I may say to another "go ahead and slap me—you have my permission." In these types of situations philosophers and others have spoken of "surrendering" rights or, alternatively and, I believe, less strangely, of "waiving one's rights." And recently, of course, the whole topic of "waiving one's right to remain silent" in the context of police interrogation of suspects has been a subject of extensive litigation and discussion.

I confess to feeling that matters are not entirely perspicuous with respect to what is involved in "waiving" or "surrendering" rights. In conveying to another permission to take a watch or slap one,

one makes legally permissible what otherwise would not have been. But in saying those words that constitute permission to take one's watch one is, of course, exercising precisely one of those capacities that leads us to say he has, while others have not, property rights with respect to the watch. Has one then waived his right in Hohfeld's strict sense in which the correlative is a duty to forbear on the part of others?

We may wish to distinguish here waiving the right to have others forbear to which there is a corresponding duty on the part to forbear, from placing oneself in a position where one has no legitimate right to complain. If I say the magic words "take the watch for a couple of days" or "go ahead and slap me," have I waived my right not to have my property taken or a right not to be struck or have I, rather, in saying what I have, simply stepped into a relation in which the rights no longer apply with respect to a specified other person? These observations find support in the following considerations. The right is that which gives rise, when infringed, to a legitimate claim against another person. What this suggests is that the right is that sphere interference with which entitles us to complain or gives us a right to complain. From this it seems to follow that a right to bodily security should be more precisely described as "a right that others not interfere without permission." And there is the corresponding duty not to interfere unless provided permission. Thus when we talk of waiving our rights or "giving up our rights" in such cases we are not waiving or giving up our right to property nor our right to bodily security, for we still, of course, possess the right not to have our watch taken without permission. We have rather placed ourselves in a position where we do not possess the capacity, sometimes called a right, to complain if the person takes the watch or slaps us.

There is another type of situation in which we may speak of waiving our rights. If someone without permission slaps me, there is an infringement of my right to bodily security. If I now acquiesce or go further and say "forget it" or "you are forgiven," we might say that I had waived my right to complain. But here, too, I feel uncomfortable about what is involved. For I do have the right to complain (a right without a corresponding duty) in the event I am slapped and I have that right whether I wish it or not. If I say to another after the slap, "you are forgiven" what I do is not waive the right to complain but rather make illegitimate my subsequent exercise of that right.

Now, if we turn to the right to be treated as a person, the claim that I made was that it was inalienable, and what I meant to convey by that word of respectable age is that (a) it is a right that cannot be transferred to another in the way one's right with respect to objects can be transferred and (b) that it cannot be waived in the ways in which people talk of waiving rights to property or waiving, within certain limitations, one's right to bodily security.

While the rules of the law of property are such that persons may, satisfying certain procedures, transfer rights, the right to be treated as a person logically cannot be transferred anymore than one person can transfer to another his right to life or privacy. What, indeed, would it be like for another to have our right to be treated as a person? We can understand transferring a right with respect to certain objects. The new owner stands where the old owner stood. But with a right to be treated as a person what could this mean? My having the right meant that my choices were respected. Now if I transfer it to another this will mean that he will possess the right that my choices be respected? This is nonsense. It is only each person himself that can have his choices respected. It is no more possible to transfer this right than it is to transfer one's right to life.

Nor can the right be waived. It cannot be waived because any agreement to being treated as an animal or an instrument does not provide others with the moral permission to so treat us. One can volunteer to be a shield, but then it is one's choice on a particular occasion to be a shield. If without our permission, without our choosing it, someone used us as a shield, we may, I should suppose, forgive the person for treating us as an object. But we do not thereby waive our right to be treated as a person, for that is a right that has been infringed and what we have at most done is put ourselves in a position where it is inappropriate any longer to exercise the right to complain.

This is the sort of right, then, such that the moral rules defining relationships among persons preclude anyone from morally giving others legitimate permissions or rights with respect to one by doing or saying certain things. One stands, then, with respect to one's person as the nonowner of goods stands to those goods. The nonowner cannot, given the rule-defined relationships, convey to others rights and privileges that only the owner possesses. Just as there are agreements nonenforceable because void as contrary to public policy, so there are permissions our moral outlook regards as without moral force. With respect to being treated as a person, one is "disabled" from modifying relations of others to one.

The right is absolute. This claim is bound to raise eyebrows. I have an innocuous point in mind in making this claim.

In discussing alienability we focused on incapacities with respect to disposing of rights. Here what I want to bring out is a sense in which a right exists despite considerations for refusing to accord the person his rights. As with the topic of alienability there are a host of concepts that deserve a close look in this area. Among them are according, acknowledging, annulling, asserting, claiming, denying, destroying, exercising, infringing, insisting upon, interfering with, possessing, recognizing and violating.

The claim that rights are absolute has been construed to mean that "assertions of rights cannot, for any reason under any circumstances be denied." When there are considerations which warrant refusing to accord persons their rights, there are two prevalent views as to how this should be described: there is, first, the view that the person does not have the right, and, second, the view that he has rights but of a prima facie kind and that these have been outweighed or overcome by the other considerations. "We can conceive times when such rights must give way, and, therefore, they are only prima facie and not absolute rights." (Brandt)

Perhaps there are cases in which a person claims a right to do a certain thing, say with his property, and argues that his property rights are absolute, meaning by this he has a right to do whatever he wishes with his property. Here, no doubt, it has to be explained to the person that the right he claims he has, he does not in fact possess. In such a case the person does not have and never did have, given a certain description of the right, a right that was prima facie or otherwise, to do what he claimed he had the right to do. If the assertion that a right is absolute implies that we have a right to do whatever we wish to do, it is an absurd claim and as such should not really ever have been attributed to political theorists arguing for absolute rights. But, of course, the claim that we have a prima facie right to do whatever we wish to do is equally absurd. The right is not prima facie either, for who would claim, thinking of the right to be free, that one has a prima facie right to kill others, if one wishes, unless there are moral considerations weighing against it?

There are, however, other situations in which it is accepted by all that a person possesses rights of a certain kind, and the difficulty we face is that of according the person the right he is claiming when this will promote more evil than good. The just act is to give the man his due and giving a man what it is his right to have is giving him his due. But it is a mistake to suppose that justice is the only dimension of morality. It may be justifiable not to accord a man his rights. But it is no less a wrong to him, no less an infringement. It is seriously misleading to turn all justifiable infringements into noninfringements by saying that the right is only prima facie, as if we have, in concluding that we should not accord a man his rights, made out a case that he had none. To use the language of "prima facie rights" misleads, for it suggests that a presumption of the existence of a right has been overcome in these cases where all that can be said is that the presumption in favor of according a man his rights has been overcome. If we begin to think the right itself is prima facie, we shall, in cases in which we are justified in not according it, fail sufficiently to bring out that we have interfered where justice says we should not. Our moral framework is unnecessarily and undesirably impoverished by the theory that there are such rights.

When I claim, then, that the right to be treated as a person is absolute what I claim is that given that one is a person, one always has the right so to be treated, and that while there may possibly be occasions morally requiring not according a person this right, this fact makes it no less true that the right exists and would be infringed if the person were not accorded it.

4. Having said something about the nature of this fundamental right I want now, in conclusion, to suggest that the denial of this right entails the denial of all moral rights and duties. This requires bringing out what is surely intuitively clear that any framework of rights and duties presupposes individuals that have the capacity to choose on the basis of reasons presented to them, and that what makes legitimate actions within such a system are the free choices of individuals. There is, in other words, a distribution of benefits and burdens in accord with a respect for the freedom of choice and freedom of action of all. I think that the best way to make this point may be to sketch some of the features of a world in which rights and duties are possessed.

First, rights exist only when there is some conception of some things valued and others not. Secondly, and implied in the first point, is the fact that there are dispositions to defend the valued commodities. Third, the valued commodites may be interfered with by others in this world. A group of animals might be said to satisfy these first three conditions. Fourth, rights exist when there are recognized rules establishing the legitimacy of some acts and ruling out others. Mistakes in the claim of right are possible. Rights imply the concepts of interference and infringement, concepts the elucidation of which requires the concept of a rule applying to the conduct of persons. Fifth, to possess a right is to possess something that constitutes a legitimate restraint on the freedom of action of others. It is clear, for example, that if individuals were incapable of controlling their actions we would have no notion of a legitimate claim that they do so. If, for example, we were all disposed to object or disposed to complain, as the elephant seal is disposed to object when his territory is invaded, then the objection would operate in a causal way, or approximating a causal way, in getting the behavior of noninterference. In a system of rights, on the other hand, there is a point in appealing to the rules in legitimating one's complaint. Implied, then, in any conception of rights are the existence of individuals capable of choosing and capable of choosing on the basis of considerations with respect to rules. The distribution of freedom throughout such a system is determined by the free choice of individuals. Thus any denial of the right to be treated as a person would be a denial undercutting the whole system, for the system rests on the assumption that spheres of legitimate and illegitimate conduct are to be delimited with regard to the choices made by persons.

This conclusion stimulates one final reflection on the therapy world we imagined.

The denial of this fundamental right will also carry with it, ironically, the denial of the right to treatment to those who are ill. In the world as we now understand it, there are those who do wrong and who have a right to be responded to as persons who have done wrong. And there are those who have not done wrong but who are suffering from illnesses that in a variety of ways interfere with their capacity to live their lives as complete persons. These persons who are ill have a claim upon our compassion. But more than this they have, as animals to not, a right to be treated as persons. When an individual is ill he is entitled to that assistance which will make it possible for him to resume his functioning as a person. If it is an injustice to punish an innocent person, it is no less an injustice, and a far more significant one in our day, to fail to promote as best we can through adequate facilities and medical care the treatment of those who are ill. Those human beings who fill our mental institutions are entitled to more than they do in fact receive; they should be viewed as possessing the right to be treated as a person so that our responses to them may increase the likelihood that they will enjoy fully the right to be so treated. Like the child the mentally ill person has a future interest we cannot rightly deny him. Society is today sensitive to the infringement of justice in punishing the innocent; elaborate rules exist to avoid this evil. Society should be no less sensitive to the injustice of failing to bring back to the community of persons those whom it is possible to bring back.

NOTE

1. Bertrand Russell, *Roads to Freedom* (London: George Allen and Unwin, 1918), p. 135: "When a man is suffering from an infectious disease, he is a danger to the community, and it is necessary to restrict his liberty of movement. But no one associates any idea of guilt with such a situation. On the contrary, he is an object of commiseration to his friends. Such steps as science recommends are taken to cure him of his disease, and he submits as a rule without reluctance to the curtailment of liberty involved meanwhile. The same method in spirit ought to be shown in the treatment of what is called 'crime.' "

B. F. Skinner, *Science and Human Behavior* (New York: Macmillan Co., 1953), pp. 115-116: "We do not hold people responsible for their reflexes— for example, for coughing in church. We hold them responsible for their operant behavior—for example, for whispering in church or remaining in church while coughing. But there are variables which are responsible for whispering as well as coughing, and these may be just as inexorable. When we recognize this, we are likely to drop the notion of responsibility altogether and with it the doctrine of free will as an inner causal agent."

Benjamin Karpman, "Criminal Psychodynamics," *Journal of Criminal Law and Criminology* 47 (1956), 9: "Basically, criminality is but a symptom of insanity, using the term in its widest generic sense to express unacceptable social behavior based on unconscious motivation flowing from a disturbed instinctive and emotional life, whether this appears in frank psychoses, or in less obvious form in neuroses and unrecognized psychoses. . . . If criminals are products of early environmental influences in the same sense that psychotics and neurotics are, then it should be possible to reach them psychotherapeutically."

Karl Menninger, "Therapy, Not Punishment," *Harper's Magazine* (August 1959), pp. 63-64: "We, the agents of society, must move to end the game of tit-for-tat and blow-for-blow in which the offender has foolishly and futilely engaged himself and us. We are not driven, as he is, to wild and impulsive actions. With knowledge comes power, and with power there is no need for the frightened vengeance of the old penology. In its place should go a quiet, dignified, therapeutic program for the rehabilitation of the disorganized one, if possible, the protection of society during the treatment period, and his guided return to useful citizenship, as soon as this can be effected."

GUILT AND SHAME

There is another way of thinking about and responding to individuals that one may find more appealing and rational than the world of guilt and a way which comes closer to what we understand by morality than the world of health and sickness. It is, however, a world devoid of moral criticism and punishment and associated moral emotions of indignation and resentment and guilt. Let us imagine set before us a description of a path to be followed. We can imagine this done by descriptions such as "the thing that is done is" or, alternatively, but to the same end, employing the concept of a model man, actual or imagined, and indicating that he manifests in his life attachment to the path. Here, when there is conduct that is not that of the path, the responses we are to imagine are those that follow upon a student's failing to work out a problem or failing to grasp a point. Invoked, that is, are the concepts of blindness, ignorance, stupidity, forgetfulness, weakness. One who fails to solve a puzzle may simply be disturbed with himself but he does not for this reason alone view his conduct as wrong. Not moving along the path is not yet knowing it or knowing it and forgetting it or knowing it and nevertheless stumbling. This world is one in which it would be natural to respond with patience, with understanding, with reminders as to how the answer is to be found. I am tempted to say that this world is analogous to that of the psychoanalyst and his analysand. What is the path? What defeats one's getting onto it? And then there are the constant reminders of the seductive byways and self-imposed blindnesses, all with the goal of aiding the person to achieve the right path, but none of it clouded with moral judgment. To be sure it is within the capacity of the individual to get on the right track, but if he is not, it is not because he has chosen to do evil. It is that he is ignorant or blind or something like that. Collapsed here, then, are the distinctions we observe between moral good and evil and men choosing the one or the other and our knowing or not knowing how to achieve

Excerpted from the article "Guilt and Punishment," in *The Personalist*, vol. 52, no. 2 (Spring 1971).

something. Would this world somehow be too pallid? Would this ubiquitous analysis of reasons for failure reveal a deficiency in one's caring for and involvement with others? This model is a fascinating one, well worth examining, I think, in some detail, but I have other matters that seem to me more pressing, however tantalizing the problems raised by this conceptual scheme. I want to move on to consider a model that has affinities with this one but which, while involving moral criticism, is criticism within a framework different from that of guilt and suffering. It is particularly in considering this alternative moral conception that one can begin to speculate fruitfully on those human propensities and those recurrent human situations that make the pull of a guilt morality so strong.

A child hits a playmate; he is told that that is a bad thing to do, that it is wrong to hit others; the next time he does it, he may be punished; he meets with "you're a bad boy." This situation, provided other conditions are met, can lead to the child acquiring the concept of a rule, his accepting a rule, and in cases of infraction feeling guilt. He may come to see that when he does wrong, punishment is an appropriate response from others. But the parent may respond differently to the conduct. He may say to the child of whose conduct he disapproves, "that is what an animal does, not a human being" and then turn away from the child. The child in such situations may come, in time, to connect "being a human being" with what is valued, with what should be sought after and connect "animal" with what is inferior, that which, when a human being manifests it, results in others turning away in disgust, turning away because they cannot stand the sight before them. The child may come, provided other conditions are met, to understand the conception of a valued or model identity, accept this and feel shame when he fails to correspond to it. We have here the seeds of a morality, let us call it a "shame morality" which, to be sure, overlaps in our own moral world with guilt, but which is still distinct. What are the features of this morality? I will now suggest a number of these.

First, conduct is evaluated through comparison and contrast with a certain model identity. "You don't find your bigger brother doing that!" or "that is what a pig would do!" It is not criticism that employs the concepts of disobeying an order or violating a rule where our critical imagery is "falling under the rule" or "being subsumed under the rule." Second, the shame morality is a scale morality not, like guilt, a threshold morality. There is the conception of a good toward which we may have travelled some distance but not the whole way. The critical concept associated with shame is failure, shortcoming, not violation. With guilt one has either done wrong or not; it is not a concept admitting of degrees of realization. Third, connected with this contrast between the conception of a scale and a threshold is the fact that with shame we may focus on failure to achieve an ideal, perfection, some maximum whereas with guilt it is a minimum demand that has not been met. Fourth, shame, unlike guilt, is not essentially tied to fault. Fault is connected with blame and blame is connected with failing to meet demands that others might reasonably place on one because they would place it upon themselves in like situations. Shame, however, may arise through failure to do the extraordinary. We may feel either guilt or shame in behaving as a coward; we may feel shame and not guilt in failing to behave as a hero. Fifth, what is valued in a shame morality is an identity of a certain kind and not, as is necessary with guilt, a relationship with others. The whole focus in a shame scheme where relationships are valued is the question "Am I worthy of being related to the other?" With guilt we have a conceptual scheme of obligations and entitlements. We have seen how this leads to the idea of owing something to others because one has taken something one is not entitled to. With shame what is crucial is a failing to correspond with the model identity. We shall feel shame, then, in situations where we do not conceive of ourselves as damaging a relationship with others. And where the maintaining of that relationship is an element in one's model identity, when one acts in a way incompatible with the relationship, the shame response focuses on failing to be a worthy person as one conceives it, rather than on failing to meet one's obligations to others and needing to restore the relationship. An act could only restore the relationship if it revealed that one was worthy of the relationship but paying a price is not alone adequate for restoration. The disposition is to be the kind of person one values. One is not forgiven one's shame and punishment does not divest one of it. Sixth, feeling shame because of what we have done, we naturally see ourselves as shameful persons and the steps that are appropriate to relieve shame are becoming a person that is not shameful. Shame leads to creativity; guilt to restoration. Seventh, shame connects with sight and guilt with hearing. What can account for this? Can it be that with shame we have a visual picture of our acting in certain ways, of our looking upon ourselves or others looking upon us and either enjoying the sight of what is seen or turning away. In guilt the "voice of conscience" speaks and we formulate in words what is to be and not to be done, words that are spoken and heard. With shame, the disposition is to hide, to vanish; with shame we want to sink into the ground, we cannot stand the sight of ourselves. With guilt the urge is to communicate, to be listened to, to confess. Eighth, shame links essentially to worth concepts and guilt does not. We may react to the shameful person with contempt; to the guilty we react with condemnation. With shame there is an inevitable derogation in one's status as a person; with guilt one's status is intact but one's relationship to others is affected. The shameful is not worthy of association; the guilty is still worthy but a price must be paid. Abandonment by others is the spontaneous result that follows upon knowledge of a contemptible nature; punishment is not a spontaneous response but a price paid for restoration. A shame morality leads to casting outside the community, exile; a guilt morality, to suffering in order to be accepted back within. We only trouble to punish those we still care about and respect. Enough, I hope, has been said in this sketch to indicate significant differences between these moralities.

We may now pose the question, given these distinct moral forms of life, what might account for our invoking or finding attractive the one rather than the other? Can we say in what sorts of settings and in what conditions guilt may come into play and where shame is less natural? Where, conversely, would one incline toward shame?

A clue here is that guilt finds a natural role within the law. It is a concept which even when employed in extralegal contexts, clearly has legal overtones. The law is concerned primarily with maintaining a certain balanced distribution of freedom and does this by ordering relationships among individuals through rules that set up a system of reciprocal rights and duties. There are a number of implications to such arrangements that provide useful leads in answering the question I have raised about guilt. First, in law our major concern is the maintenance of a minimum level. Second, the concern is that conduct, relating to values sought to be protected, reach a minimum. Third, relatively precise guides and rules are seen as assuring maintenance of the distribution of value in the community. Fourth, there is recognition that strong inclinations operate against compliance and there is need for incentives. Fifth, there is an absence of concern with motives, with purity of heart, grandeur of soul. Diminishing harm to others is the predominant goal. Sixth, there is incentive put forward for restoring relationships. Finally, the relations are between individuals who do not ordinarily have close ties that would, apart from obligations or a sense of obligation, provide strong motives for satisfying the interests of others. It is, I think, whenever interests of this kind predominate that one is pulled to responses that generate the conception of guilt. It will be, for example, when we view as pre-eminently important a certain balanced distribution of freedom that we shall think in terms of rights and duties and move to concepts of wrongdoing and guilt. Shame will arise when our concern is achieving more than a minimum, when our concern is that individuals realize to the fullest what they have within them, when what one is takes priority over a nice balance in relations with others with respect to particular types of conduct.

THOMAS SZASZ AND *THE MANUFACTURE OF MADNESS*

Thomas S. Szasz, a practising psychoanalyst, in a series of books,[1] most recently *The Manufacture of Madness*, argues that the concepts of madness and sickness are being systematically misused. It is his view that the concept of madness has become bloated beyond recognition, that it is now commonly applied to those who are merely "different" or "odd" or whose views differ from our own. We have gone in for "madness mongering." Underlying this misapplication is a more fundamental conceptual error productive of great social evil. We have come to conceive of madness as a form of sickness, where being sick is defined as having something painful happen to one, being afflicted from without. Cases of madness do exist for Szasz—for example, cases involving serious and extreme deviations from acceptable norms of behavior and processes of reasoning such as aggressive paranoia—but there is no mental illness. The phrase "mental illness" is, for him, an oxymoron. And it is viewing madness as sickness that leads to a constant manufacture of madness, that is, its expansion over territory previously claimed for the hegemony of human responsibility, territory where man chose between good and evil and was an autonomous agent not a helpless victim.

Why is there no such thing as mental illness? Szasz argues that mental illness is a myth, or, as he sometimes writes, "a metaphor" or "a fiction" or "an erroneous concept." He never settles on a single way of describing its suspect character, but it is apparent that the standard case of illness or sickness or disease (no attempt is made to suggest any significant difference among these concepts) is a *physical disease*. Syphilis affecting the brain would be such a disease. But there are *functional disorders*—for example, the wide assortment of psychoses such as paranoia and schizophrenia—that are not, in his judgment, essentially connected with any physical disease. And there is, finally, in the three-fold classificatory scheme he adopts, *social deviancy* such as homosexual conduct. Only the first class, physical disease, is properly speaking a disease. The

Reprinted from *UCLA Law Review*, vol. 18, no. 6 (1971).

latter two abnormalities, functional disorders and social deviancy, are failures to meet problems of living. If we ask what underlies this conceptual view, Szasz answers that functional disorders and social deviancy make implicit reference to political, social, or legal norms and that absent in these cases is any generally agreed upon physical criterion of "abnormality."[2] He believes that he can conclude that saying "what we call mental illness is not a disease is like asserting that two and two makes four. . . ."[3]

What has accounted for the conceptual error? What evils have resulted? What steps must now be taken? To each of these questions Szasz has answers as provocative as his denial that mental illness exists. With extraordinary persistence, imagination, and insight, with irritating exaggeration and disquieting suggestiveness, he traces, particularly in *The Manufacture of Madness*, the villainous role assigned mental disease in the elemental drama of master and slave. To label one as sick permits us to "take care of him," to make decisions affecting his liberty under the guise of giving him help. Mental disease, he argues, now plays the role earlier assigned to witchcraft. Employing force and fraud, always masked, of course, by a rhetoric of benevolence, society with the enthusiastic complicity of psychiatrists, disarms and disposes of the unwanted and the threatening in a way which allows it to feel both justified and uplifted. Szasz presses forward with a number of troubling analogies between witchcraft and mental illness. Both concepts are "imprecise and all-encompassing . . . freely adaptable" to whatever use one wishes to put them.[4] With both witchcraft and mental illness the classes constantly expand, encompassing diverse groups, sharing only this: they are unwanted and seen as threats. With both, the motive for society's conduct is said to be benevolence but what is done is horrifying; lobotomy, shock treatment, and indefinite incarceration replace burning. With both, those who have expertise in recognizing symptoms gain in power, prestige, and wealth. With both, denials of the alleged status serve to confirm for the experts the initial suspicion. The protest, "but I'm not sick," becomes itself evidence of sickness. Finally with both, critics of the system reveal by their very criticism symptoms that permit their classification as witches or mentally ill. The institutional psychiatrist, then, the psychiatrist prepared to use force and fraud in the service of the family or the state, has taken over from the priest of the Inquisition. He conquers souls for medicine and thereby serves not his involuntary patient but those who seek to destroy the patient. People today won't talk of witchcraft; but they eagerly accept the diagnosis of mental illness of those whom they find strange or threatening or with whom they disagree.

There is much of great value in Szasz's analysis of the nature and role of mental illness. I am convinced that what he calls "a semiotical analysis of psychiatric operations,"[5] is a fruitful way to proceed. This approach asks, for example, what the hysteric means to convey by his symptoms and thus places those symptoms in the category of expressions in a language.[6] His discussion of the manipulative aspects of sickness—how those who take on the role of the ill and those who impose it may have power over others as their primary object—is filled with insight. He makes the familiar point that turning ourselves into cripples allows us to demand things from others that we should find difficult to demand otherwise. And treating another as a cripple allows manipulating them, for their own good, as we should otherwise find hard to justify. He is also right in claiming that to think of one's difficulty as a disease requiring treatment by an expert may hinder rather than promote needed change. Viewing ourselves as responsible for the pain that we experience is certainly essential, in a wide range of cases, if we are to change and if the pain is to disappear. And, finally, it is evident that labelling someone mentally ill has serious implications for the person's status and liberty. On all these important matters I think Szasz's emphasis and observations are right on target. Ironically, and sadly, he falls prey to some of the very faults he charges to others. He goes wrong in failing to set out and give sufficient weight to the apparent connections between the concepts of physical illness and so-called mental illness. In going wrong here, he finds it easy to impugn the motives of psychiatrists and he betrays a tendency to bloat beyond recognition the concept of responsibility; he goes in for "responsibility mongering" in his eagerness to respond to "madness mongering."

Szasz errs in failing to give sufficient attention to what pulls people, even people not apparently interested in power over others, toward the view that functional disorders are a form of sickness. It is true, as Szasz insists, that the operation of the will in much so-called mental illness is greater than its role in, say, disease of the brain. The will may on occasion even play its part in bringing about a disease of the brain, as when, for example, a person takes certain drugs with full knowledge of their injurious effect on brain tissue, but generally brain disease resembles other diseases of the body such as cancer in that the will of the person is unrelated to the disease he has. Suffering in much mental illness, on the other hand, is more closely connected with choice, because it is a pattern of response to situations the person perceives as painful. We naturally think that a person's goal is to avoid suffering by living in a world that is more satisfying than the real one. But, though we may be inclined to regard mental illness as self-imposed and to perceive that the will of the sufferer may have an inevitable part to play in his cure, it is still important to take in the significance of a person's describing himself as in the grip of something alien to him. In some cases the analogy to bodily disease is quite close. A person suffers from some physical symptom for which no physiological explanation is available, perhaps an uncontrollable twitch. After discussion the psychiatrist may provide his patient with an insight that leads quickly, perhaps immediately, to the symptom's disappearance. Here, through insight, freedom from affliction is acquired in much the way a medical practitioner might liberate one from pain. More common are the cases in which some fundamental change in the person, a change in habits of thought and feeling and conduct, is required. But even here it is not simply that the person is disabled and suffering that pulls toward the concept of sickness. The person may feel shackled and unable merely by some act of will to rid himself of suffering. Until the self-imposed blindness is faced and overcome, the person will remain as he is. We may be responsible for the habits we have and we may bear ultimate responsibility for changing them; but it may nevertheless be true that, having the habit, we are unable to change by exertion of will any more than we can rid ourselves of a disease of the brain by exertion of will. It is, then, the operation of habits of various kinds that leads to our sense of being bound and to the thought that we are in the grip of something alien and it is this, conjoined with the need for some assistance from the outside, perhaps more than anything else, that accounts for thinking in terms of illness.

Though Szasz has a casual way of impugning the motives of psychiatrists, his most significant failing is that his way of looking at things idealizes the responsibility of the mad. He deprives the concept of responsibility of some of its discriminating power by refusing to distinguish between the responsibility of the mad—even the completely mad—and the sane.

There are two ways to make an all-out assault on a concept such as responsibility. One approach is to claim that the concept has no application. "No one is responsible." The other, more subtle way, is to claim that the concept applies to everything. "We are all responsible all the time." Szasz travels too far along the latter route and thereby makes less serviceable the very concept whose integrity it is his object to preserve. He does with responsibility, then, what he charges others with doing with sickness. This comes out clearly in one of his major arguments for abolition of the defense of insanity:

> In the Anglo-American (and also Roman) philosophy of law, ignorance of the law is no excuse. How can a person ignorant of the law be held responsible for breaking it? How can he be blamed for committing an act that he did not know was prohibited? The answer is that the well-being of a free society is based on the assumption that every adult knows what he may and what he may not do. *Legal responsibility is an expectation:* first, that people will learn the laws of the land; second, that they will try to adhere to them. Thus, if they break the law, we consider them "blameworthy." If we apply this reasoning to offenders who are alleged to be mentally ill, similar conclusions will be reached. If mental illness resembles bodily illness, it will not excuse them from adherence to the law. If, on the other hand, mental illness is similar to ignorance (as indeed it is)—then again it is not a condition that excuses violation of the law. Just as the recognition of ignorance and its correction are the responsibility of the adult citizen, so also are the recognition of mental illness and its

correction. Thus, from a purely logical point of view, there are no good grounds for the rule that there should be two types of laws, one for the mentally healthy and another for the mentally sick.[7]

At least two comments need to be made about this astounding passage. The first relates to its unquestioning acceptance of the principle "ignorance of the law is no excuse." If a man makes efforts to ascertain the law, efforts that we should judge those of a reasonable man in the circumstances and yet fails in his attempt, it would be a moral wrong to punish him for violating a law with which he believed in good faith he was complying. The principle of respect for individual freedom of choice, so venerated by Szasz, would be infringed if the man were punished. Second, Szasz places on all those whom we might classify as mentally ill the burden of discovering their condition and taking steps to correct it. This is weird. We might expect a blind man to realize his condition and take extra precautions in his social dealings because of it, but there would be something strange in expecting this of an idiot. Shall we impose upon him the burden of recognizing his idiocy and taking precautions appropriate to it? It is the same with certain classes of mental illness. To be sure, a person might feel himself inexplicably pulled toward doing harmful things to others despite his apparent desire not to do them. He might think, "I'm a kleptomaniac and I'd better get help." There is force in the claim that such a person should be held to the same degree of responsibility as one who suffers from some physical affliction and who because of it is expected to take appropriate precautionary steps. But surely there are others whose extraordinary habits of thought and feeling of long standing and pervasive effect have impaired their capacity to view accurately either themselves or the world around them. Are we guilty of some gross conceptual error and inhumanity when we seek to reflect sensitivity in our criminal law to those cases in which a man's capacity to appreciate what he is doing is substantially diminished? In the interest, then, of keeping within respectable limits the concept of illness, Szasz has so extended the boundaries of responsibility that he partially destroys the very thing he wishes to preserve, a meaningful concept of human responsibility. If mental illness is a myth, what shall we label the claim that all madmen are completely responsible?

Szasz falls prey to another fault that he has charged to others. He writes that "today is not a propitious time in human history for obscuring the issue of man's responsibility for his actions, by hiding it behind the skirt of an all-embracing conception of mental illness."[8] Man, he insists, must confront problems of living, problems of good and evil, and he must not suppose that assistance can come from without in the form of a cure if he fails. Excellent. But there are ways and ways of avoiding responsibility. If the hard choice is made to appear simple, we mask the character of what we face and relinquish responsibility by subtle maneuver—perhaps not all responsibility but some. This tendency is at work in Szasz and derives from his seeing sharp lines where in fact there are fine gradations. This can be seen most clearly in his treatment of involuntary commitment.

Our practice in this country is to permit involuntary commitment because of mental illness under a variety of conditions, absent any proof of crime. In some jurisdictions it is sufficient that the person adjudged mentally ill be a danger to himself or others; in other jurisdictions mental illness along with a finding of need for care and treatment is sufficient; in still others the legislation requires that the person be mentally ill and that his welfare or the welfare of others requires commitment.[9] There appear a variety of possible justifications for these legislative criteria. First, it might be thought that mentally ill persons are more dangerous than the broader class of ascertainably dangerous persons. Second, it might be thought that the mentally ill do not know their own interests, and that commitment will aid them in making this discovery. On this view, it is benevolence that explains why mental illness joined with evidence of a danger to oneself justifies commitment. Third, the mentally ill might be thought to be less than fully autonomous agents. Thus, in interfering with them we do not perpetrate the evil we should were we to interfere with a free agent capable of rational choice.

Whatever the criterion or combination of criteria for commitment, the situation is one that should cause alarm, for even where mental illness and danger to others are conjoined as a test for commitment, it is obvious that the possibilities for injustice abound. The vague concept of danger (What kind of danger? To what degree of probability?) is joined with the even vaguer concept of mental illness to guide decision-making in a setting where commonly few, and sometimes none of the procedural safeguards attending criminal trials are present, and where commitment involves loss of liberty, deprivation of a host of political and civil rights, dreadful stigma, and a not particularly encouraging prospect of successful therapy. It is a good thing, a very good thing, that the veneer of benevolence be stripped from our institutions and that we look hard at what is being done in the name of helping people. Where I find Szasz wanting on this subject, to which he has made enormously valuable contributions, is in his cavalier treatment of a core issue, the difficult dilemma posed by our need to strike a balance between the risk of restraining responsible persons whose commitment is undesirable and the risk of not restraining persons whose commitment is desirable. Szasz's position can best be examined by considering his views on suicide.

Szasz proposes that all involuntary commitment be abolished except for two emergency categories. The first is that of the passive, stuporous person who may be looked upon as an unconscious medical patient. We can restrain him until he awakes. The second class is that of the aggressive paranoid who threatens violence and for whom no ordinary jail is appropriate. Strikingly omitted from these categories are the suicidal. Why should we forbear from interference here? Because we cannot arrogate to ourselves knowledge of what is in another's best interests; each man must assume responsibility for his own life and death. Now it may well be that much evil in this world has come about through interfering with people "for their own good" but Szasz seems content with leaving the matter there. It is a point that needs to be made, but at the beginning of discussion and not as the only discussion.

A person may sometimes be blind to his own best interests and we are guilty of no lack of respect for him if we interfere, despite his protests, with what he wishes to do. Our friend's wine has been drugged and we observe him climbing out the twentieth-story window. Of course we stop him and do so despite his vehement protestations that he wants to die. Or, again, our friend may have drunk more than he can decently hold. He, not another, is responsible for his condition, but while in it, he is not himself as he climbs out the window, protesting he wants to die. Again, we may surely interfere. A person may also be blind to his own interests through lifelong habits of thought. May not interference also be justified in the case of such persons as it is with the drugged person? Can we not restrain in the hope that with time and talk—not limitless of course—some calm and rationality will gain ascendancy in such persons? We have, then, a difficult problem. It is always dangerous to substitute one's own judgment for that of another on the question of what is good for him. In some cases we believe that it is wrong to interfere even though we think the person blind to his own interests. In other cases we think it right to interfere. Where shall we place the blindness of the mad? Where shall we place it when their mistake may be irremediable as it is when life may be taken? Though I draw lines in these cases, I do not find it easy to do so. And I do not find particularly helpful observations such as: "—the individual must be free to abjure liberty; were he not, he would have no liberty to abjure."[10] What is absent in Szasz's treatment is a sufficiently sensitive appreciation of how difficult here is our choice between good and evil. In giving the impression that it is easy, he escapes full responsibility, one thing he knows we always do at too great a cost.

When we learn that a psychoanalyst believes that mental disease does not exist, that psychiatrists are power-hungry servants of the dominant elements in society, that the defense of insanity and involuntary commitment must be abolished to avoid crimes against humanity, we may find ourselves falling into a trap laid by the pervasive ideology condemned by Szasz. We may think: He must be mad. With that facile thought we can avoid seriously confronting what he has to say. The temptation must be withstood. Szasz's catalytic observations have thrown light where before there was too little or none. His great virtue, one that excuses for me all the exaggeration and seemingly deliberate perverseness, is his storming bastions of complacency and dogmatism, holding before us constantly the ideals of individual liberty and human dignity, and demanding of us re-examination of our ways of thinking, feeling, and acting in the light of these ideals.

NOTES

1. *The Myth of Mental Illness: Foundations of a Theory of Personal Conduct* (1961); *Law, Liberty, and Psychiatry: An Inquiry into the Social Uses of Mental Health Practices* (1963); *The Ethics of Psychoanalysis: The Theory and Method of Autonomous Psychotherapy* (1965); *Psychiatric Justice* (1965); *The Manufacture of Madness: A Comparative Study of the Inquisition and the Mental Health Movement* (1970).

2. See Thomas Szasz, *Law, Liberty, and Psychiatry* (New York: Macmillan Co., 1963), p. 14. "The concept of illness, whether bodily or mental, implies deviation from a clearly defined norm. In the case of physical illness, the norm is the structural and functional integrity of the human body. Although the desirability of physical health, as such, is an ethical value, what health is can be stated in anatomical and physiological terms. What is the norm deviation from which is regarded as mental illness? This question cannot be easily answered. But whatever this norm may be, we can be certain of only one thing: *viz.*, that it must be stated in terms of psychological, ethical, and legal concepts."

3. Thomas Szasz, *The Manufacture of Madness* (New York: Harper & Row, 1970), p. 112.

4. Ibid., p. xix.

5. Thomas Szasz, *The Myth of Mental Illness* (New York: Hoeber-Harper, 1961), p. 137.

6. Ibid., p. 12. "Hysteria is nothing more than the 'language of illness' employed either because another language has not been learned well enough or because this language happens to be especially useful."

7. Szasz, *Law, Liberty, and Psychiatry*, p. 132.

8. Ibid., p. 16.

9. For a comprehensive discussion of the various statutory schemes regulating involuntary hospitalization see Chapter II of *The Mentally Disabled and the Law*, ed. F. Lindman and D. McIntyre (1961).

10. Thomas Szasz, *The Ethics of Psychoanalysis* (New York: Basic Books, 1965), p. 76.

HERBERT FINGARETTE AND
THE MEANING OF CRIMINAL INSANITY

I

Legal insanity has been exhaustively treated in legal literature, but apart from the provocative view that there is no such thing as mental illness and the equally provocative suggestion that the defense of legal insanity be abolished,[1] there has been a preoccupation with formulations of the test of criminal insanity at the time of the criminal act. M'Naghten[2] is criticized and defended; new tests appear on the scene and meet in their turn with support and scorn. Two large, philosophically exciting topics have met with neglect, or, if not neglect, surprisingly cursory treatment. First, all tests of legal insanity make some reference to disease of the mind, but there is no generally accepted definition of this condition. Not until McDonald[3] in the innovatively oriented District of Columbia Court of Appeals did a Court attempt to provide a definition for use by judge or jury of this concept; philosophically inclined theorists have largely avoided examination of the concept.[4] Second, while contemporary developed systems of criminal law make provision for the defense, there is, as yet, no clearly articulated and persuasive rationale offered for it. We are, instead, proffered language that captures our intuitions and little more: "it would be unfair to hold the insane responsible." If this response is challenged, we may meet with the suggestion that it would be unfair for precisely the reasons it is unfair to punish someone whose involuntary bodily movements have caused harm or, alternatively, to punish someone who was mistaken with respect to relevant facts (summoning to mind mistaking a human being for a tree). It is evident that neither of these claims will withstand scrutiny, for there are those generally acknowledged to be insane and insane so as to be exempt from responsibility who have

---

*Herbert Fingarette, *The Meaning of Criminal Insanity*, (Berkeley, Los Angeles, London: University of California Press, 1972). Page references are to this work.

Reprinted from *Inquiry*, vol. 17 (1974).

complete control of their limbs and who do not make the mistake
of taking one object for another.

It is the chief merit of Fingarette's study* that these two neglected
topics are made his central concern; what is most novel and
exciting in his study relates to these issues; and I restrict my own
discussion to his treatment of them. Fingarette attempts, first, to
provide an analysis of the concepts of insanity or mental disease
and criminal insanity. He then offers a rationale for the defense of
insanity which moves beyond our intuitions and avoids the too
facile conflation of the defense of insanity with absence of
voluntariness and ignorance. If we possess a clearer idea of the
nature of insanity, a clearer idea of the nature of criminal insanity,
we can, so far as he is concerned, utilize any of the three tests
presently most discussed in the United States provided that
whichever test is used is clarified by a gloss derived from his
analysis.[5]

The book, then, whatever we might conclude to be its value for
those concerned with the practical administration of the criminal
law is, unlike most other writing on the topic, philosophically
stimulating, for it offers, despite some familiar contemporary
philosophical warnings, a definition of insanity and a rationale for
insanity as an excuse.

II

How does Fingarette define insanity?

1. Insanity is (a) irrational conduct (b) from grave defect in the
person's capacity for rational conduct (c) which is at least for the
time an inherent part of the person's makeup.

If we now substitute for the terms "rational" and "irrational" the
central meaning of those terms as developed in the earlier
discussions, we derive:

2. Insanity is failure to respond relevantly to what is essentially
relevant by virtue of a grave defect in capacity to do so inherent at
least for the time in the person's mental makeup.

Since 1. and 2. make it plain that where there is insanity there is
inherent incapacity to respond relevantly, it is evident that:

3. So far as there is insanity there cannot be responsibility (p. 203).

Criminal insanity is grounded on this:

The individual's mental makeup at the time of the offending act was such that, with respect to the criminality of his conduct, he substantially lacked capacity to act rationally (to respond relevantly to relevance so far as criminality is concerned). (p. 211)

Fingarette's analysis is intended to reflect what he regards as the prevalent intuitions that insane conduct is irrational conduct and that an insane person is an irrational person. To be sure, not all irrational conduct is insane conduct, but Fingarette's conviction is that all insane conduct is irrational and all insane persons are, at least with respect to the area of their insanity irrational. What then is irrationality?

Our attention is first drawn to a gradation in what he labels the "strength" of senses of rational and irrational. Fingarette's quarry is that sense of "irrational" invoked when we describe insane persons as irrational. On his gradation of senses it is the "weakest" sense of irrational that is relevant. The strongest sense of rational for him, implies proof and demonstrability. A slightly weaker sense is roughly synonymous with "sound, sensible, wise, judicious, well thought-out." There is a still weaker sense (the one that connects with insanity) such that foolish conduct may still be labeled rational, for a person may have "his reasons and though they be few or poor reasons, even this paucity of reason precludes saying he is irrational, out of his mind" (p. 185). A man, Jones, described as rather unintelligent, not much given to thoughtful reflection, concerned more with his needs and wishes of the day or week rather than great ventures spanning long periods, goes off to the races with a few extra dollars earned in the hope of making a killing.

We may think of him with tolerance or with scorn as simpleminded, foolish. But we would hardly argue that in living that way he shows he is irrational—where "irrational" is intended to suggest "craziness, bizarreness, being out of his mind." (p. 185)

Again, to behave without any reason at all, say, to behave with caprice, needn't be irrational. A man who lifts a stone and for no particular reason hurls it into the wind may do so for "no reason at all" and not be irrational. Further, a man may be malicious and not irrational. He concludes that there is a weak sense of "rational" such that each of the persons in these examples is rational, but there is still another sense in which the insane person is not. What is then present in these cases and absent in cases of insanity?

In all of the above, while we might speak of irrational conduct, there is still a capacity to respond relevantly to essential relevance. Where, however, an individual lacks this capacity, and his conduct is related to the incapacity, we have irrational conduct in the weak sense of "irrational" introduced by Fingarette, the sense in which insane conduct is irrational. The sense of "rational" Fingarette introduces to illustrate insanity, then, relies on the concept of capacity for rational conduct. All cases of irrational conduct in his weak sense will then imply an irrational person in his weak sense of "irrational," for irrational conduct in this sense reflects an impairment in the capacity of a person. Fingarette provides several imaginary cases to help our understanding of this suitably weak sense.

Consider first a man who is quite inebriated, so much so that he is unable to grasp "even the physical implications of what he is doing." Jones, our inebriate, perceives Smith, hurls a rock at him, but he is

> in fact unable to respond because of his mental state, to the relevant physical consequences of his act. Jones was in this respect acting irrationally. He did indeed act crazily, as one who was "out of his mind" (though this would not be the same as saying he was literally insane or mentally deviant) . . . he was incapable of responding to the relevant personal, moral, and legal aspects of his situation. (p. 187)

The core concept of "essential relevance" is provided its most elaborate description by Fingarette in his discussion of this case:

> . . . the harm, the suffering, the wrongness and the criminality of the harm if committed purposely—all emerge as relevant to what Jones is about to do. These implications are not possibly

relevant; their relevance is not peripheral or subtle. This is all obvious, demanding, rudimentary, plain. I shall speak of such relevance as essential relevance. (p. 186)

The next case to aid in our understanding of "irrational conduct" is one in which Jones is

> incapable of responding to the relevant emotional-moral aspects of the situation and his conduct . . . he is emotionally flat and does not respond to the relevance of human suffering . . . he just has no capacity to react. The suffering of others, in its emotional-moral relevance, is beyond his ken. . . . Insofar as humane, emotional, moral features of a situation are relevant to his conduct Jones is irrational. (p. 188)

Fingarette distinguishes such a person from the "professional criminal" who has the capacity to respond to the essential relevance embodied in the law. His response while illegal is relevant, for he is after gain for himself.

Fingarette next introduces irrationality in the sphere of volition. Jones is now a heroin addict in the throes of intense withdrawal symptoms and in a state of craving for heroin and in desperate need for cash. He apprehends the physical and emotional, moral and legal aspects of the situation but

> he finds that he cannot respond relevantly to those. He is uncontrollably animal-like in his assault. . . . The physical quest to grab Smith's money is the sole relevant factor to which his behavior is responsive. . . . Given the circumstances as described, Jones must be judged to be acting irrationally; he has lost control over himself and in this respect has lost his reason. (p. 190)

In his final example, meant, I assume, to correspond to our image of a paranoid, Jones has a false belief about being pursued and persecuted. He is someone who

> cannot genuinely respond relevantly to anything pointing to the falsity of that belief. . . . If we believed Jones genuinely considered and took into account what was relevant, we would view him as mistaken or stubborn. But the gross discrepancy between the belief he holds and the relevant facts as we see them, the fanatic character of his belief in the face of

everything, lead us to conclude that in this connection he is incapable of rationality, not merely a dedicated or stubborn man who is in error. (p. 191)

Fingarette concludes his analysis by drawing distinctions between the non-rational and the irrational and between the insane and those who are irrational in the weak sense but not insane. He first distinguishes those who are not rational from the irrational, children, say, from the irrational. He claims "we typically reserve the appellation 'irrational' for those who would normally be rational but who have lost their reason. Irrational thus has inherent implication of pathology, aberration from the normal" (p. 191). Again, "of a being that we did not think of as normally having a capacity for rationality, we would not say that it acts irrationally but that it is non-rational" (p. 194). The next task is to distinguish the irrational person from the insane person, for our imaginary inebriate above is not regarded as crazy. Fingarette claims that to be insane the lack of capacity must be a part of an individual's nature and not merely a temporary effect of special circumstances; the condition must be "characteristic of the autonomous working of his mind," "a relatively enduring part of the individual's makeup" (p. 197).

This is the substance of Fingarette's ambitious attempt. Even if we grant, what I believe is not adequately demonstrated, that there is an essential connection between insanity and irrationality, Fingarette's discussion of irrationality in the weak sense that is needed to elucidate insanity is left obscure and because of this, the difficulty we have in making articulate and precise the nature of insanity now shifts to irrationality. The sources of my difficulty relate to each of the key concepts introduced to elucidate insanity: (1) impairment of capacity; (2) relevant response; (3) essential relevance; (4) mental make-up; and (5) "one whom we would normally expect to be able to act rationally."

III

I have, first, some observations about his treatment of capacity. In criticizing the *McDonald* definition of mental disease or defect

Fingarette claimed "nor are there any criteria offered for application of the boundary term "substantially" (p. 33). It is nowhere made clear to me how his own formula "he substantially lacked capacity to act rationally" is immune from precisely the same criticism. There are several different and difficult issues here. There is, first, of course, the vagueness of "substantially" and the inevitable problems we shall have in applying any criterion relying on it. This is perhaps unavoidable. What is striking is that in each of Fingarette's illustrations of failing to respond relevantly to essential relevance no mention was made by him of the incapacity being grave or substantial; it was that each of the individuals was unable to respond. Why does he qualify by writing of "grave" and "substantial" when formulating his final definition? There are several possible ambiguities here. Is it that Fingarette wishes to draw our attention to the fact that irrationality often operates over a limited area? Or is it rather that given a certain area in which one is irrational, one's capacity for rationality is gravely impaired? I think it fairly clear that Fingarette, while being prepared to acknowledge that one needn't be crazy about everything, principally had in mind the latter type of case. But then another ambiguity may strike us. Is the impairment "grave" in the way in which one's capacity to see may be thought to be gravely impaired, implying that no effort will allow one to see better? Or is it that it is impaired in the way that capacity is impaired when a choice is seen as particularly difficult as in cases of a starving man grabbing another's food or in cases of duress. I don't find an answer to this question in Fingarette, though my guess is that he might incline toward the impairment of vision analogy when thinking of cases such as paranoia and the difficulty of choice model when thinking of cases in which impairment of volition is the basis of a claim of irrationality (the family of cases that includes his heroin addict). If we focus upon the cases to which the impaired vision analogy might be thought appropriate, we need to understand how we are to take "substantially impaired" with respect to them when really what is at issue is presumably a fairly rigid belief structure such that the individual either disregards contrary evidence or so construes the evidence that it invariably confirms one's beliefs. I might say "Jones' vision is substantially impaired" and imply that he simply cannot see an object at a certain distance which Smith, who has normal vision, can quite clearly see, or I might imply that Jones' vision is such that he only vaguely, in a blurred manner, makes out objects that Smith with his normal vision quite clearly makes out. Now how would we go about applying this model to beliefs? Are we to say the paranoid, for example, simply cannot appreciate that certain evidence is contrary to his beliefs? If so, why not just say he is unable to grasp essential relevance? Or are we to say he has moments during which he questions his beliefs because of the evidence before him and yet, despite the inconsistency with his beliefs, he still keeps to them? And to take care of this possibility we talk of "grave impairment." But then why should we excuse such a person? He presumably now is someone who would have grounds for believing he might be wrong in his beliefs and is to some degree aware of those grounds. I do not find an answer to this question in Fingarette. Until we get some illumination on this issue, we may have an impression that his words have clarified matters for us but find when we come to apply his formula to actual cases that we are as perplexed as ever.

If Fingarette means for us to take the "difficulty of choice" rather than impairment of vision model—and some cases of psychological disorder may suggest this model's applicability—other problems arise. Why is it that when insanity accounts for substantial incapacity for rationality we should excuse, but not if starvation or an upsurge of anger does? It is also clear that the view of some is that substantial impairment, even if caused by mental disease, should mitigate but not excuse.[6]

Next, I must confess to not yet being persuaded that, for insanity generally, there is any greater incapacity for rationality, at least as Fingarette defines rationality, than when insanity is not present. Individuals may hold religious beliefs or hold beliefs and have attitudes shaped by social and cultural conditions with a rigidity that belies any suggestion of capacity genuinely to consider evidence, so that they would seem to have in some respects an impairment of capacity for a relevant response to essential relevance equally as grave as that of the insane. Fingarette is, of course, aware of such cases. He refers to "quasi-religious sects" and writes

> Such borderline vagueness of the test is not a cause for suspecting it but, rather, for strengthening one's confidence in it as a bona fide formulation of our intuitive concept of insanity. It is just such borderline bizarre conduct and beliefs that intuitively are most difficult to classify with respect to sanity or insanity. This *is* at the borderline of our concept of rationality. (p. 243)

I am not sure why Fingarette limits his observation to "*quasi-religious sects,*" for it would appear that we could have a clear-cut case of a religious sect composed of individuals who from our point of view hold bizarre beliefs and behave, again from our point of view, strangely. Even if we should think of individuals as irrational in these contexts, and I have strong doubts that we appropriately can, I am not sure we are on the border of the concept of sanity. I think Fingarette has gone wrong on this issue and wrong because he gives to the *capacity* for rationality too great a weight and fails to elaborate for us sufficiently the concept of pathology which is also linked on his analysis to being insane. It seems clear that we do not classify as insane individuals from other cultures who behave, from our standpoint, in abnormal ways and who have rigid belief systems. It will be recalled that in distinguishing the non-rational from the irrational Fingarette claimed that we reserve "irrational" for those whom we normally expect to be rational and who are not. I believe that it might have been useful for him to elaborate that formula in connection with distinguishing those classes of persons incapable of rationality who are thought of as insane from those who are not. Such an analysis would bring out the connection that classifications of insanity have with social norms and being a member of a particular group and, further, the close connection between insanity and some malfunctioning defined in the light of certain norms. But even this formula—what we "normally expect" of someone—if invoked here, causes problems. It is one thing to say that animals and infants are non-rational rather than irrational because we reserve the concept irrational (in the weak sense) for those "who would normally be rational but have lost their reason" (p. 191). It is another to invoke this concept to establish that adult individuals with certain religious convictions and cultural backgrounds are not insane.

Fingarette needs, I believe, to elaborate his discussion of those conditions that defeat an attribution of being crazy given an acknowledged incapacity for rationality as he understands that concept. My guess here is that insanity may be one of those concepts such that a number of criteria are relevant to its application—capacity for rationality may be one of them—but that there are other criteria whose presence, even given lack of capacity for rationality, would defeat an attribution of insanity. For example, just the fact that a system of belief is socially reinforced may disincline us in labeling one who subscribes to it as insane.

IV

I turn now to difficulties I have with Fingarette's conception of a relevant response. The case used to illustrate this concept is that of the heroin addict. The addict's conduct, according to Fingarette, is irrational because of an inability to respond relevantly in accord with his perception of the essentially relevant norms. This claim is connected with the one he makes about the malicious person, for there, it was argued, the person is still regarded as rational because of the presence of a capacity to respond relevantly to relevant moral norms. I think something has gone seriously wrong here. What is it? Both the addict and malicious person, whatever their capacity to respond relevantly to essential relevance as it involves the interests of others, are responding to an interest of their own. Given our concept of rational conduct, is there anything of greater essential relevance? The addict is described by Fingarette as "animal-like" in his behavior. But of what significance is that? The addict might not have acted in animal-like fashion but nevertheless claimed an incapacity to behave otherwise. His situation would then be roughly comparable to those who are starving and steal to allay their hunger. In these cases, we judge the agent's rationality not by a capacity to respond to relevant social norms but by virtue of a capacity to take into account their own interests or pressing needs. Again, an individual might be intensely egocentric and the judgment might be "there is little chance that that person will ever really care about anyone but himself." Is this person—whom we might regard as immoral—also irrational—and not just irrational but insane—just because of an impairment in the capacity of the kind described? Non-acceptance and inability to respond emotionally to values of one's own group is not, I believe, made out by Fingarette as a sufficient ground for a claim of irrationality or insanity.

Fingarette has too quickly moved from the fact that an individual is unaware of or ignorant of certain matters to the conclusion that the individual is acting irrationally if he responds to the situation as he erroneously construes it. Is the inebriate who throws the stone irrational given the situation is as he construes it? Would a person who hallucinated a monster because of the effect of some drug and who then took appropriate steps to destroy the monster be acting irrationally? Hardly. Why is the affectless person in Fingarette's example irrational if others really do not matter to him? If they do not matter, is not the conduct perfectly rational? The paranoid is not irrational given what he believes; and it does not follow that, because there is some ignorance at the source of it all, this implies irrational conduct. These doubts of mine imply that I am unconvinced by Fingarette that (a) a substantial impairment in capacity for a relevant response to essential relevance, as he defines those matters, implies irrationality and that (b) insane persons who are "out of their minds," "who have lost touch with reality" are necessarily irrational.

The addiction case deserves still additional attention before we move on to a closer look at the concept of essential relevance. With the addict we have, for Fingarette, an irrational person engaging in irrational conduct in the suitably weak sense. Is such a person insane? It certainly does not accord with our intuition to say so, but how does Fingarette distinguish such a case from insanity? He does not, regrettably, devote attention to this matter. His basis for distinguishing such a case from insanity may go off on the concept of "mental make-up" though he says nothing about what bears on something being part of one's mental rather than bodily make-up and gives the impression that addiction is illustrative of the class of things of which insanity is a part. The addiction case also raises another issue that it would have been worth Fingarette attending to. He acknowledges in the case of the inebriate that we might hold the inebriate responsible for harm done while in the incapacitated state because of the presence of capacity at some earlier time, presumably at the commencement of drinking. But it would then appear likewise compatible with fairness to hold insane persons responsible, perhaps particularly in that area of cases introduced by Fingarette under irrationality with respect to volition. Why should they not be charged with failure to take reasonable precautions? There is no discussion of this not implausible symmetry, one that suggests that being insane at the time of one's conduct is not by itself, any more than being unconscious or inebriated at the time of conduct, a sufficient basis for exculpation.

V

Several of the difficulties I have so far set forth with Fingarette's analysis tie in with his concept of "essential relevance." He says remarkably little about this concept central to his theory. I have the uncomfortable feeling that what may be at the heart of this vague concept does not come out in his discussion. The insane may seem to us out of touch with reality—though I confess to a doubt that it is necessarily to any greater degree than with the so-called sane—and while something like "essential relevance" may be tied to the concept of reality, what are we to understand by that concept? My sense is that much craziness—I would scrupulously avoid offering a formula to account for all cases—is basically losing touch with the reality that is one's self, with being in a condition that leads to conduct that is perplexing, not just to others, but to oneself, with engaging in conduct that is over a wide range of cases without satisfaction for oneself. When a person goes mad one strong pull we often—not always—have is to think of that person as fundamentally different from what he was before the advent of the madness. It is this which may in part account for the terrifying prospect of going mad. It is a form of death. More particularly, my sense is that with certain classic cases of insanity we have the following conditions satisfied: (1) there is a set of beliefs arrived at not by confrontation with what is normally regarded as evidence for such beliefs but rather as having its source outside rational reflection by the agent; (2) the beliefs are relatively immune to change through confrontation with evidence controverting the belief; (3) the false beliefs mainly involve beliefs about oneself— who one is, what one values, where one is, what is the appropriate course of conduct for one given one's values, etc.; (4) there is a form of incoherence between either one's conduct and one's beliefs about what is valuable or between the false beliefs one has about oneself and the other beliefs one holds. It is the third and fourth points, if they have validity, that Fingarette chiefly neglects. Thus, when we claim that someone has lost his mind, my intuition on the matter is that we may be struck by a discontinuity in the person's identity, that this discontinuity is not the result of any deliberate choice, and that it leads to ways of thinking and acting that are malfunctional given our conception of the person prior to the onset of the false belief system. I do not offer these comments with any firm conviction of their adequacy but only to convey my impression that there is more to insanity than Fingarette's formulas and examples bring out.

VI

Now, if my criticisms of Fingarette's analysis and these intuitions have some merit they may have a bearing on issues of responsibility in ways which, while not incompatible with Fingarette's account of the non-responsibility of the insane, are nonetheless different. He emphasizes the pointlessness in holding responsible those who are not responsible agents. I sense more may be involved. First, our practice of holding persons responsible operates so as, characteristically at least, to condemn those who put their own interest before the interest sought to be protected by the law. If we have a class of cases of individuals who characteristically are not self-interested in their behavior, and many of the insane are not, we are, I think, hard put to blame or condemn. Second, if the point about discontinuity of identity has validity, the principle of exculpation that might be called into play would be one that precludes holding responsible an individual who is not, through no fault of his own, the self-same person as the one responsible for the wrongdoing. Third, our inclination to excuse an individual may sometimes be accounted for by that individual's being markedly different from us, "an alien" to our way of life. It is not that the individual is irrational; it is that, given reality as we believe it to be, the individual is not in touch with it, and because of this we deem it strange to apply concepts meant for those essentially like us. My sense is that those labeled "psychopaths" pull us in this direction.

Whether or not these suggestions as to possible grounds for exculpation are convincing, I would want to express doubts that some single explanation of the sort Fingarette provides can adequately account for our attitudes in all cases in which we confront individuals whom we think are out of their minds. It is the old story: we may ourselves lose touch with reality if we accept some simple formula with the belief that it captures the rich variety of the world.

NOTES

1. See Thomas Szasz, *The Myth of Mental Illness* (New York: Hoeber-Harper, 1961); H. L. A. Hart, "Changing Conceptions of Responsibility," in *Punishment and Responsibility* (Oxford: Oxford University Press, 1968).

2. *M'Naghten's Case*, 8 Eng. Rep. 718 (1843).

3. *McDonald v. United States*, 312 F.2d 847, 850 (1962): "Mental disease or defect includes any abnormal condition of the mind which substantially affects mental or emotional processes and substantially impairs behavior controls."

4. Two noteworthy exceptions are: J. Feinberg, "What Is So Special About Mental Illness," in *Doing and Deserving, Essays in the Theory of Responsibility* (Princeton, Princeton University Press, 1970); B. O'Shaughnessy: "Mental Structure and Self-Consciousness," *Inquiry*, vol. 15, nos. 1-2, (1972), pp. 30-63.

5. *M'Naghten*: The party is to be adjudged insane if "at the time of the committing of the act, the party accused was labouring under such a defect

of reason, from disease of the mind, as not to know the nature and quality of the act he was doing; or, if he did know it, that he did not know he was doing what was wrong."

Durham v. U.S., 214 F. 2d 862 (1954): "An accused is not criminally responsible if his unlawful act was the product of mental disease or mental defect."

Model Penal Code (American Law Institute) § 4.01 *Mental Disease or Defect Excluding Responsibility:* "(1) A person is not responsible for criminal conduct if at the time of such conduct as a result of mental disease or defect he lacks substantial capacity either to appreciate the criminality of his conduct or to conform his conduct to the requirements of law."

6. *English Homicide Act*, 1957: "(1) Where a person kills or is a party to the killing of another, he shall not be convicted of murder if he was suffering from such abnormality of mind (whether arising from a condition of arrested or retarded development of mind or any inherent causes or induced by disease or injury) as substantially impaired his mental responsibility for acts and omissions in doing or being a party to the killing. . . . (3) A person who but for this section would be liable, whether as a principal or as accessory, to be convicted of murder shall be liable instead to be convicted of manslaughter."

3 Guilt and Suffering

I

WE associate being guilty and feeling guilty with pain, with pain inflicted upon us by others, and pain that we inflict upon ourselves. The verdict in a court of law is "guilty," and this by itself may make for suffering. Anxiously awaited is the sentence and this may provide still another blow. Will it be our freedom or our life? Having either taken away means still more pain. There are also those times when we may return a verdict of guilty against ourselves, and believing that we are guilty we may begin to feel guilty. It is a painful state. Reflecting upon it we may fasten onto the view that our responses to ourselves when we judge ourselves guilty and feel guilty mirror responses of others to us when they judge us guilty. We may think of "the bite of conscience" and the picture before us then is that of a man turned against himself, a man making himself suffer, a man resembling a scorpion. More than this, the man who feels guilty often seeks pain and somehow

Reprinted from *Philosophy East & West*, vol. 21, no. 4 (October 1971).

sees it as appropriate because of his guilt; indeed, the feelings of guilt may disappear and the man may connect their disappearance with the pain he has experienced. When we think of what it is to feel guilty then, we think not only of painful feelings but of something that is owed; and pain is somehow connected with paying what one owes.

Reflection on being guilty and feeling guilty may lead to the view that there is a logic of guilt, that there are rules that, among other things, guide us in determinations of guilt and innocence, determinations of the conditions under which it is and is not appropriate to feel guilty, determination of the conditions under which feeling guilty is no longer appropriate. It is a logic whose guidelines we often unthinkingly and unconsciously follow, a logic that certainly appears to connect guilt in some intimate way with pain and suffering.

Some philosophers have argued that while this logic is perfectly rational, it does not apply to man. Others have argued that, for one reason or another, it is an irrational logic. Some attack guilt from within and some from without. Among those in the first group are philosophers who would accept the appropriateness of determinations of guilt and conventional responses to it were there moral fault and were it discoverable. They have argued, however, that we cannot ascribe moral fault to human beings. The reasons for this are various and well known. Some hold that all choice is strictly determined; others that the model of sickness and health covers human conduct; others that all so-called moral wrongdoing is really a species of ignorance and not a knowing choice between good and evil; and still others that fault, if it exists, cannot be discovered. Here familiar arguments are deployed to demonstrate deficiencies in our knowledge of any one of a number of matters essential to a determination of guilt, for example, deficiencies in knowledge of the mind of others, knowledge of one's own mind, knowledge of a person's identity over time by others and himself, knowledge of the past. These general philosophical positions may remind us of more particular cases, cases in which we absolve a person of guilt by claiming "he is not to blame; he did his best to avoid harm," or "he is not the same man who did it," or "how can we blame him not knowing for sure what was in his mind when he did it?"

This essay has little or no relevance to these and other philosophical positions that challenge the appropriateness of determinations of guilt by questioning the existence, or our knowledge of the existence, of one or more features essential to a person's being guilty. What I have to say is relevant to a group of interconnected critiques, some philosophical and some not, that challenge the logic of guilt itself.

Of critical importance is the complaint that the logic of guilt requires suffering because of what is past and that to suffer oneself or to make another suffer because of what is past, is to impose suffering for its own sake, and this is irrational. Justification for infliction of pain, if ever there is justification, must lie in the future. We shall here, I think, be reminded of those familiar and interminable disputes between retributivists and utilitarians, those who look to the past for justification of punishment and those who look to the future. Connected with this point is the charge that feeling guilty implies a cowardly attitude toward one's past deeds, an unwillingness to let go of the irretrievable and face the future. Instead of accepting that what is done cannot be undone, the guilty frantically attempt to undo. For the courageous there are no erasures. Closely connected with this is the claim that one must forget in order to live, that one must leave behind what is behind, and that attachment to a painful past is a form of enslavement that prevents man from standing upright. What guilt creates, for persons who argue in this way, are creatures who are weak, self-conscious, apologetic, hesitant, and crippled. Further, guilt operates within an essentially mercantilistic framework. Its logic is that of "tit for tat"; it requires acts that "square accounts" or "even the score" or "pay off the debt"; and it leaves matters, when restoration succeeds, in the sorry state they were in before the conduct giving rise to guilt. It is then argued that something essential escapes the crude grid of guilt, something, indeed, that thinking in terms of guilt makes it all too easy to escape. There are those who would add to this indictment the charge that guilt fails to serve the very purposes for which it apparently exists, for determinations of guilt and the suffering that follows because of it only give rise to further hatred, rancor, and anger, or give rise to the very things that occasion guilt in the first place. Guilt commences a cycle of pain not easy to break. Guilt also makes for passivity; it makes for people accepting what is unacceptable. Suffering that should be despised and struggled against is seen as deserved, as punishment for wrongdoing, and there is acquiescence where there should be rebellion. Finally, there are those who remind us of the role of guilt in the tragic human game of manipulation where arousing guilt is a particularly effective means of gaining domination over others.

I think we shall feel force in some or all of these criticisms. These various assaults on guilt also, I believe, shall leave us with inner turmoil, for we may think there is guilt and there is guilt, some irrational and some not, of some we, perhaps, should wish to be free, of some not. But there may be this turmoil because a certain note is sounded in these criticisms that makes us feel unsure of what about guilt we find acceptable, and what about it we find unacceptable even where it is not being misused, even where, given its logic, guilt clearly applies. Why, we may wonder, cannot bygones be bygones? Why cannot we just forget the hurt done to us and the hurt we do to another? Does it make sense that we should suffer because of what is past? It may not appear so. Still, if we turn attention to the man without a conscience, without a sense of guilt, the man dominated, as Bentham claimed of us all, exclusively by pain and pleasure for himself alone, we may question whether this man is as we wish to be; and we may feel certain that we should not be at ease with him around. We may think of the psychopath and think that guilt is the price we pay for something in human life we are unprepared to sacrifice, a concerned involvement with others.

There is something, then, about guilt, perhaps its connection with pain and suffering for what is over and done with, that leads us to be suspicious and perhaps critical of it. But there is also something about guilt, its connection with caring for others, perhaps, too, its connection with caring for ourselves, that may lead us to think it essential to human life as it should be.

What I write here is addressed to this tension in the attitudes some of us may have toward guilt. My aim is to obtain a better grasp of being guilty and feeling guilty and the connections between these concepts and pain and suffering. With this we shall perhaps have a better idea of what about guilt we are prepared to say is acceptable and what about it is not. I first set out a theory of wrongdoing. I then go on to say what it is to be guilty of wrongdoing. I next examine what it is to feel guilty and elaborate in some detail the connections between this concept and pain and suffering. Then there is brief discussion of certain restorative conditions and pain and suffering. Finally, I offer some tentative conclusions on the limitations of a guilt framework and speculate on the topic of guilt and time.

There are a number of topics very closely connected with what I undertake to examine that are left almost or entirely untouched without, I hope, dreadful consequences. I do not spend time on unconscious guilt or neurotic guilt or the sense of guilt which is forward looking, captured by the phrase "the dictates of conscience." Nor do I bother with whether or not there are distinctions, be they subtle or otherwise, between feeling guilty and feeling guilt. Nor do I work out the complicated and fascinating relations between feeling guilty and judgments of guilt.

II

We are guilty of wrongdoing. What is wrongdoing? I approach this question by asking: What are the features of a world in which the concept of wrongdoing has application? I sketch a case that I think central for the application of this concept, but I draw attention to other important cases of wrongdoing that do not neatly fit my description of the central case.

The world in which wrongdoing has application is one, first, in which individuals place value on certain things. When individuals are deprived of what they value, they view themselves as injured, hurt, pained, and they suffer. If we did not possess the concept of being harmed, we would not think in terms of wrongdoing.

It is, next, a world in which individuals have inclinations which, if given in to, would generally lead to grievous injury to others. The concept has its principal application in situations where individuals are related to each other through the possibility of injury to others. The concept of wrongdoing applies in cases in which one injures oneself, cases in which one intends to injure another, cases of trivial injuries, and cases in which one injures animals. I believe in all such cases certain features are lacking whose absence may incline at least some to say that the concept of wrongdoing does not apply.

Next there is the conception of some limit on conduct, a limit sometimes expressed, particularly in legal and quasi-legal settings, in the form of a precept or rule which is seen as ruling out certain conduct, as making certain conduct not eligible. Sometimes the connection between the idea of a limit and what is valued is very close, and we say that certain conduct is wrong just because it injured another or damaged what was valued. Sometimes the connection is less close, and we say that conduct was wrong just because it manifested disregard of a precept or rule. In either case certain conduct is seen as not eligible to one. The existence of this conception implies that individuals for whom the limit is a guide have a capacity for choice and a capacity to choose in the light of their appreciation of the significance of the limit. If the world were seen as one in which all conduct followed from antecedent causes as do movements during an epileptic seizure, there would be no point to the existence of such a conception. This would also be so if individuals were viewed as unable to appreciate the significance of a limitation upon conduct.

When the limit assumes the form of a precept or rule it is viewed as imposing a duty of compliance upon all those to whom it is applicable. It is correlated generally with the concept of an entitlement or right to demand compliance. Failure to comply constitutes disobedience or violation. In central cases of intentionally committing an act known to be wrong, it is not merely that something has been done that one was not entitled to do, but more significantly, one is seen as taking what does not belong to one. The domain of what is not eligible to one is the domain of goods that one has no right to possess. With central cases of wrongdoing one is seen as possessing, then, what one has no right to possess. This conceptual fusion of doing and taking, a fusion that makes concepts resembling those of property and theft central to wrongdoing derives, I believe, from conceiving satisfactions acquired through a wrongful act, the satisfaction attendant upon relinquishing the burden of self-restraint, and the satisfaction attendant upon achieving the object of one's desires, both as objects illegitimately seized. But, further, if we possess the concept of a limitation upon conduct, we see as appropriate a range of responses to individuals who do and do not conform to the limit. Pressure to conform and negative responses in the event of nonconformity are marks of the existence of a limit upon conduct. If there were no hostility in case of its disregard and instead favorable responses or indifference, we should naturally question the existence of such a limit. In like manner we judge that a person has abandoned his property if we observe no dispositions on his part to use it or to prevent its use in any manner by others. The presence and absence of certain conduct and attitudes here is the mark of something being eligible that was not before. But it is also the case that the negative responses are mediated by the conception of the limit. The existence of a precept or rule or the wrongness of one's injuring another is cited or implied in the criticism of the person. Where conduct is seen as wrong and not just hurtful, the reactive emotions of persons incorporate some reference to the conception of a limitation on conduct, to certain conduct not being eligible; not anger alone then, but indignation and resentment, not regret alone then, but feeling guilty.

The limit on conduct is seen as setting some threshold or minimum of attainment; it is not an ideal to be attained. There will be those who are looked upon with admiration or awe because they accomplish for others or themselves what few can accomplish, but failure to behave as these extraordinary individuals do is not seen as wrongdoing. Wrongdoing is failing to reach a level of attainment that individuals generally are seen as able to satisfy.

When we possess the concept of wrongdoing, I want to suggest that it is connected for us with the concept of "being joined together" with another or others, the idea of union, the idea, too, that in this union one is complete, one is whole, in a way that one would not be without it. Being a member of a community, being friends, being lovers—all imply union as I employ this concept. This union and completeness are valued. When they exist there is, among other things, sharing of and commitment to the same values and because of this one is the recipient of approval, benefits, warmth, and favors associated with the relationship. More than this, the concept of being complete is connected in our understanding with being able to function as one would not be able to were one in some way incomplete, just as one would not be able to function entirely as a man were one not to have arms. When one is guilty of wrongdoing, one separates oneself from another or others with whom one was joined. Wrongdoing, then, is typically conduct which, if joined with fault, gives rise to guilt and separation from those with whom one was joined. Those who are not viewed as within this union may be viewed as dangerous, but their conduct is not seen as wrongdoing. They may be controlled; they may be reacted to as we sometimes react to wild animals, but they are outside the world of wrongdoing with its implications of separation and union.

Next, wrongdoing arises in a world in which there is a conception of righting the wrong. It arises in a world in which persons possess a conception not just of separation from others but of coming together again with them, a conception of mending what has been torn, repairing what has been damaged—restoration. Wrongdoing then arises in a world in which asking for and receiving forgiveness, making sacrifices, reparation, and punishment exist; and where they, as well as other responses, have the significance of a rite of passage back to union. And so it is characteristic of individuals who possess the concepts of wrong-doing and righting the wrong that they remember injuries and that they connect certain present feelings and conduct with restoration of relationships damaged by past conduct. A wrong, then, is not understood as righted when matters are simply where they were before the wrong because forgetting may account for this, and forgetting is not a restorative response. For restoration there must be a bringing back by certain appropriate responses which carry significance for the parties. It is this feature of wrongdoing, the possibility of righting the wrong, of a coming together again, that makes entirely understandable the inclination that individuals may have to structure situations so that they may feel guilty rather than some other way, a way that, because restoration is thought impossible, may be more painful than feeling guilty.

Finally, some words of caution. While conduct that is injurious to others is central to the concept of wrongdoing, it is important to note that certain relationships can be damaged by an individual's having a certain state of mind alone, a state incompatible with the relationship as it may be defined and valued. An intention to do an act that would betray a friend, for example, is itself a state that damages the relationship between the friends. Further, the spirit in which an act is done, the motives that underlie it, and the feelings we do and do not have, though normally disconnected from determinations of the wrongfulness of an act, may be relevant to the issue of whether or not a relationship has been damaged if the relationship is conceived of in such a way that it can be damaged by these states of the person. In some of these cases because fault is present, in only an attenuated form, there may be a pull in the direction of the concept of shame. Next, there is a distinction to be drawn between doing what is wrong and being guilty of wrong-doing. There are cases in which one does not do what is wrong. Sometimes another is responsible for wrongdoing; or one does not *do* anything, for example, one was unconscious at the time; or what one did caused injury, but it was justifiable injury. But there are cases in which there is wrongdoing, but one is not guilty despite responsibility in some sense, because one was, for example, reasonably mistaken. To summarize, there is no wrongdoing if one is not responsible for wrongdoing. But one may be absolved of guilt though responsible for wrongdoing. To be guilty of wrongdoing implies fault. Given wrongdoing and fault there is guilt. What state is that?

III

The central, though not the only, case of being guilty of wrongdoing is one in which one is both at fault and responsible for wrongdoing and thus is separated from others, obligated to them, and deserving of some hostile response from them. I say this case is central, for I believe that the concept is employed here with its full panoply of associated concepts, concepts such as being guilty before another or others, asking for and gaining forgiveness, and mending what has been broken. It is otherwise with cases in which one is guilty of wrongdoing with respect to animals, unless, of course, one conceives of them in certain atypical ways, and it is otherwise in those cases in which one has departed from some personal code and no damage to a relationship with another has been caused.

To be seen as separated implies that one's wrongdoing has ruptured one's union with others. Of course one may injure another, even injure in a way that requires reparation, and not have thereby damaged a relationship. To be seen as owing something to others implies that something must be given up if the relationship is to be restored. Before one can be joined with others, an obligation must be discharged; in the revealing and, yet, I fear, also misleading, legal imagery coloring our thought about guilt, the debt must either be paid, exacted, or forgiven. To be seen as deserving of an unfavorable response implies recognition that when one damages what others value, others are entitled to feel resentment or indignation, to complain, to condemn, or to be hostile.

IV

We are now in a position to consider connections that pain has with the concept of being guilty of wrongdoing. First, the concept of being guilty of wrongdoing has application in circumstances where there is a point to having the conception of a limit upon conduct. Limitations presuppose human inclinations to behave otherwise and thus they demand sacrifice of satisfactions. Peace, it is sometimes said, is purchased at the cost of the instinctual. When this is said it is recognized that sacrifice of the instinctual, whatever might be thought its beneficial consequences, involves sacrifice of satisfaction. Further, it is generally the case that individuals who relinquish the burden of self-restraint meet with responses that displease them. The mark of the existence of a restriction on conduct is a cost imposed for its disregard. But now I think that more progress may be made by turning attention to "feeling guilty."

"Feeling guilty we feel bad." We think this statement very likely true, for reflecting on the ways we have felt when feeling guilty we may recall thinking that we felt rotten, depleted of energy, and tense. I shall have something to say about feeling guilty as a species of feeling bad. But now let us ask, supposing we do feel bad, what are the sources of this feeling? First, we may, of course, when feeling guilty, feel bad because someone for whom we care has been hurt; their being pained pains us. It would be similar, then, to the pain that we should feel were they struck down accidentally by a falling tree or afficted with a disease.

There is, next, the pain that comes from separating ourselves from the union that we value. To be cut off from what we love is intensely painful, and the pain of separation involved in guilt resembles this. But there is more involved, for I have suggested that in union, best exemplified in love, there is an intensely satisfying feeling of wholeness or completeness. In seeing oneself as cut off from others one feels a sense of incompleteness, as a lover who loses a loved one may feel that a part of him has been taken away or torn from him. The person feels that peculiar pain and uneasiness when feeling guilty of cutting off a part of himself. He feels what he may wish to describe as a division within himself, and this feeling is understandable, for if one feels guilty one defines oneself partly as someone joined with another or others. In cutting oneself off from others one comes to see oneself as being cut off, not whole, as if one had destroyed what one loved and thus also destroyed a part of oneself. This image of cutting off and being cut off, not whole, finds support in our view of the guilty person as not being able to function as a whole person could and does, not being able to enjoy life fully, being as it were cut off from experiencing the world in satisfying ways.

The feeling bad derives from antagonism toward oneself because one has acted against what one is attached to, and this antagonism feeds the feeling that one is divided within oneself. There is hostility toward anyone who attacks what is cherished. In feeling guilty one experiences the pain associated with the judgment, "it is my fault." So the feelings of indignation that a person would have directed against another had that person been at fault in causing hurt to those for whom one cared are directed against oneself.

The feeling bad derives also from a tension to do something. One typically feels as if there were some burden of which one must rid oneself, as we say, of the weight of guilt. This may have several explanations. It may sometimes derive from a sense that one possesses something that one has no right to possess. In some cases of feeling guilty we have preferred to satisfy our own desires at the expense of others. There is the need to give up the satisfaction we have obtained, and there is tension within us until we are relieved of guilt. Even in cases where this is not so, cases involving some inconsiderateness and hurt where the person feeling guilty does not see himself as having acquired satisfaction, there will be a pain that derives from the longing to leave the state of separation and hostility toward oneself and be joined together. To feel relieved of guilt is to feel again that one is joined together with others and with oneself, to no longer be divided within and at war with ourselves and others. This need to make amends, to mend what has been damaged, and to be at one again with others and oneself is at the core of guilt. If it is successful, it is atonement, being at one with.

These sources of pain in feeling guilty suggest close connections that feeling guilty has with caring for others and caring for oneself. Part of what it means to care for another is feeling pain in circumstances where another is pained. And part of what it is to care for oneself is to be pained at the hurt done oneself by the hurt done others. Not being pained by the hurt done others would reveal an absence of care for them and an absence of care for oneself as a person identified as caring for others. And not ever being pained by the hurt others do one or the hurt one does oneself is to reveal a complete absence of care for oneself. A mark, then, of care both for oneself and others is the pain experienced when one hurts another or oneself.

When feeling guilty, I have suggested, we feel badly. Feeling guilty is partly defined by its being a painful condition. It is also a condition in which we are said to "suffer"; sometimes it is said that in this condition "we suffer pain." To say of someone that he is suffering or suffering pain, as I shall understand it, implies something about the person's attitudes and dispositions with respect to what has significance as pain for the person. It implies that the person is not disposed to have the experience, that the person does not have a favorable attitude toward the experience, and that the person does not delight in or relish or enjoy or get satisfaction from the pain itself. It is possible to say, "I am feeling pain," or "I am experiencing pain" and to go on to say "and precisely because I am I feel good; I'm not suffering in the least." Just as some people seem to delight in the fact of others being pained, we are all aware that some seem to delight in the fact that they are experiencing pain. We are most ready to accept the distinction between experiencing pain and suffering pain when painful sensations are being enjoyed. Those other cases, with which we are also familiar, in which one derives satisfaction from being rejected or insulted by others or having one's prized possessions destroyed, are ones where we may be less inclined to speak of deriving satisfaction from pain, for we may feel a pull to say in such cases, "the person isn't experiencing any pain." Still, even in these situations a person may derive satisfaction from reflecting on his painful experiences occasioned by these various injuries done him. He indeed may lose the thrill of satisfaction if the vividness of the pain leaves him. We need now to introduce a distinction between experiencing pain and suffering pain, for examination of the range of connections that pain has with feeling guilty makes it apparent that persons who feel guilty and who either have pain inflicted upon them or inflict it upon themselves characteristically derive satisfaction from the pain. There is something about the person who feels guilty that may remind us of masochism.

When feeling guilty we characteristically suffer pain that is partly constitutive of the feeling. But pain connects with feeling guilty in at least two other ways that require attention. First, it is associated with certain spontaneous expressions of feeling guilty. Second, it is associated with restorative responses that may relieve one of feeling guilty. Common to both, the pain that is expressive of feeling guilty and the pain that is connected with restoration, is a characteristic absence of suffering. One's attitudes and dispositions toward pain in these situations are unlike one's characteristic attitudes and dispositions toward the pain constitutive of feeling guilty.

There is pain essentially connected with restoration and pain not essentially, though characteristically, connected with restoration. The pain essential to restoration involves feeling a certain way; one's heart, we may say, must be in a certain painful state, and this pain is like the pain constitutive of feeling guilty in that it is relatively disconnected from choice even when compared with the pain that we may unthinkingly inflict upon ourselves in the expression of feeling guilty. But it is only relatively disconnected from choice, for it is a pain that we may be responsible for bringing about in a way that we are not ever responsible for bringing about events absolutely disconnected from choice. We can bring about a condition of our heart, but we cannot bring about our immortality. The pain not essentially but characteristically connected with restoration is more closely connected with choice than is the pain that is associated with the expression of feeling guilty, for it is pain quite deliberately chosen; and it is a pain that does not characterize a condition of one's heart. I shall try now to put some flesh on these ideas.

Pain is associated with the expression of feeling guilty for at least three reasons. First, it is expressive of hostility toward oneself. The pain may be inflicted as spontaneously and nonpurposively as the slap we give ourselves immediately upon awareness of having done something stupid. The characteristic expression of anger is destructiveness. Second, pain inflicted upon oneself is a characteristic expression of one's conviction that one possesses what one has no right to possess. Where what is illegitimately possessed is some satisfaction, giving this up typically takes the form of inflicting pain upon oneself. Third, expressive of one's longing to have whole what was damaged is confession. This is associated with pain, for typically what we confess to is something which, had we been observed in the act, would have caused in us shame. When we confess, we may attempt to mitigate the pain of shame by not facing the other party.

In expressing one's feelings when feeling guilty one may strike oneself and one may confess. In doing these things one causes pain for oneself and characteristically also acquires satisfaction in doing what one does in expressing one's feelings. Contrasted with pain that enters into restoration, the pain connected with the expression of feeling guilty is not valued because of its painful character and the significance this has for one's feelings about oneself and one's feelings about and commitment to a damaged relationship. In the one case we get satisfaction expressing our feelings, and the expression involves pain. In the other case we derive some satisfaction precisely because it is pain we are experiencing. Confession, for example, when expressive of our feelings involves pain as a by-product; confession, when it is restorative, is found partly satisfying because it is something that involves pain. Let us now turn to the rich topic of restoration and pain as connected with it.

V

Feeling guilty we feel badly. It is also sometimes said that the mark of feeling guilty is the need for punishment. Some think punishment "evens the score" and restores what has been damaged —"he's paid his debt to society." Sometimes it is even said that the "pangs of conscience" are punishment, and we can understand this pull, as I have said, for a prevalent image of the man who feels guilty is a man turning on himself because of a belief that he has done wrong. Further, as there is a pain associated with the expression of feeling guilty, there is temptation to see this pain as punishment. Punishment is of course an extremely elastic concept and a social practice with a highly overdetermined justification. Still, the pain we suffer when feeling guilty and the pain involved in the expression of these feelings differs from pain that is inflicted with the significance for us of punishment.

Central to punishment of others, I believe, is a communicative act. It is not punishment as we ordinarily understand it if one simply deprives another of something of value, even if this is done because of some wrongdoing, if one does not attempt to make apparent to the person who has been deprived the connection between the deprivation and wrongdoing, that one is being deprived because of wrongdoing. Punishment is deprivatory conduct that means something, and we seek to communicate its meaning to the person being punished. The pain associated with feeling guilty, while a response to the belief that one has done wrong, is not a pain that one inflicts upon oneself with the significance carried by punishment inflicted by others. It is not, in general, deliberately inflicted pain as requital for wrongdoing. Of course pain is sometimes deliberately sought out as punishment by a person who feels guilty, and, indeed, even the pain constitutive of feeling guilty can bear significance as punishment. There is a cycle in which a person may punish himself for one wrong by committing another and feeling guilty because of it. What is sought out is the pain of feeling guilty as punishment for wrongdoing. Indeed, a person may tenaciously hold onto feeling guilty over some wrong done, and the pain constitutive of this feeling can then, also, take on significance as punishment.

Punishment by itself is never, I believe, restorative of close relationships defined by feelings and attitudes, though in highly structured social situations its infliction may be viewed as restoring a certain disrupted rule-established equilibrium of benefits and burdens. Punishment is a common response to wrongdoing in nonreciprocal, parent-child relationships and in impersonal, recip-rocal legal situations. The role of punishment is nonexistent, insignificant, or positively perverse in contexts where moral wrong is done a stranger or where a friendship or love relationship based on affection, respect, and trust has been damaged.

The preeminent role of punishment in legal settings is accounted for by a variety of factors: (1) the interests protected are of a recognized high order of importance; (2) the absence of close personal ties precludes the possibility of general reliance on motives that subordinate one's own strong inclinations to the interests of others; (3) the parties injured by conduct in violation of the rules cannot generally be expected to contain hostile impulses or be forgiving; (4) there is, as compared with close personal relationships a greater risk that regret, sorrow, and disavowal are not associated with recognition of wrongdoing and a greater pressure to incapacitate the wrongdoer and prevent further wrongdoing; (5) there is need for the system to convey the genuineness of its commitment to the proscriptions; (6) there is need to maintain assurance for those who voluntarily comply with rules that others will not gain an unfair advantage over them by being able with impunity to relinquish the burdens of self-restraint.

Spontaneous expression of anger of course is compatible with the existence of close personal relationships. Infliction of punishment by the injured party upon the other party has a peculiar inappropriateness. For one thing, punishment would sound an unappealing note of moral arrogance. But we must also wonder, of what use would it be? The person who views the pain he has caused another either responds as a friend or lover would or he does not. If not, what is essential to the relationship, a condition of one's heart and mind, will hardly be brought about by punishment. If the person responds as a friend or lover would with pain and renewed commitment to the relationship, the injured party, if a friend or lover, responds with forgiveness. So, while punishment might be seen as restoring a rule-established equilibrium of benefits and burdens by taking from the wrongdoer benefits not permitted him, it is never by itself restorative of relationships that are defined by feelings and commitments. Something must come in these relationships from the injured party if ever there is to be restoration— forgiveness. But something of course must also come from the guilty party, and it is to this party's restorative responses that I now turn.

There is, I claimed, a pain essentially connected with and a pain not essentially but characteristically connected with restorative responses by the guilty party. The pain not essentially connected is the one that is chosen. It takes forms such as self-punishment and sacrifice. There is an explanation for pain playing so prominent a role in these restorative responses. Where there is some object that has been taken it must be returned, or where there is physical harm done something must be forthcoming that serves to aid mending. In either case we are giving up what we ordinarily wish to have. But there is something more. By inflicting upon oneself something painful or by accepting its infliction on one, one thereby provides both oneself and the other party with a sign of the hurt one feels in having hurt the other, a sign of one's recognition that one possesses what one should not, and a sign of one's present commitment to the relationship. The satisfaction that one obtains in self-inflicted or accepted pain here comes from the very character of the conduct as painful, for it is this that evidences how much what has been done counts for one and how much it means for one to restore. When doubt has been raised about care and commitment, assumption of pain is a preeminent mark of their presence. Care for another, commitment to another, imply being prepared to sacrifice one's interests in avoiding pain, at least to some extent, to another. The man prepared to sacrifice his life for a woman gives a proof of love that a man who refuses to sacrifice does not give, and gives a proof, too, which is not yet available if no occasion for sacrifice has arisen. Indeed, part of what it means to love another, as well as oneself, is not only pain felt when the loved object is hurt but pain one is prepared to face for the loved one. Therefore, in a genuine restorative response there may be a satisfaction derived from restoring, a satisfaction derived from giving something to one for whom one cares, and a satisfaction derived from experiencing pain, for this makes apparent how deeply hurt one has been by the damage and how deeply committed one is to the relationship.

We may be reminded of occasions when gifts were given and hard feelings eased. But unless the gift is seen as involving some extraordinary sacrifice or effort or assumption of extraordinary burdens, it does not, even though it is the doing of what one is not obligated to do, evidence as does something painful the inner condition of the person and the genuineness of his commitment. Among the reasons for this is perhaps the expectation that persons in such relationships are already disposed to convey to the other what they are not obligated to convey.

This pain that plays a role in restoration is pain that I have claimed is characteristically, but not essentially, present. Dispositions to assume what is painful must be there, but there need not be actual assumption. It seems clear that sometimes "forgive me" coupled with what is expressive of the hurt felt in hurting another gains forgiveness. Indeed, in close personal relationships, where the parties pride themselves in a deep understanding of each other, there may be forgiveness and the capacity to accept it without evidence provided by one party to the other party of pain, or, indeed, by the other party of forgiveness.

The pain that is essential to restoration is not deliberately chosen. The pain constitutive of feeling guilty is essential to restoration, and it is normally not deliberately chosen. But there is another pain, not deliberately chosen and not constitutive of feeling guilty, but of a closely connected state, that seems also essential to restoration. I think it is a condition of the person captured by the concept of feeling contrite. This feeling combined with repentance provides the conditions for forgiveness. If there are the outward signs without what is supposed to be signified, one element for genuine restoration is absent; forgiveness purchased by fraud does not constitute restoration. Where forgiveness from another is not forthcoming for one reason or another, contriteness and repentance are among the conditions that allow for forgiveness of oneself.

A person who feels guilty may not be disposed to say, "I'm sorry" or "Forgive me"; he may not feel sorry about what he did.

And he may not be prepared to disavow his act and commit himself to not doing it again. He may be neither contrite nor repentant. A person feeling guilty might suffer and also take satisfaction in doing what he did. There might be pride over what was done. We need only think of the young boy who disobeys his father and who, while feeling guilty, also looks upon himself with more respect. He feels guilty but prefers being damned to renouncing his act. The pain constitutive of feeling contrite is sorrow or sadness because of one's guilt. Our image is that of a person humbled by contemplation of his wrong, a person who feels smaller than before, a person prepared to react to infliction of pain and forgiveness with acceptance and absence of resentment and defiance. It is both the condition of feeling contrite and of being repentant that are signified by the pain that is deliberately chosen to evidence the hurt we feel and the genuineness of our commitment to a relationship. They constitute those conditions of heart and mind that typically allow for restoration.

VI

Anything deserving to be described as "a moral way of looking at the world" takes the past seriously. We certainly take the past seriously when we think in terms of guilt. Surely the grudge that some have against guilt cannot be that it implies that we remember and see significance in what is remembered. Nor can it be that when we respond to what we remember with pain felt and pain chosen that something is basically amiss, for pain marks our care for ourselves and for others. To be entirely forward looking would reflect negatively on the presence of feelings and dispositions that define for us valued relationships between persons. If the logic of guilt is vulnerable, it is not, I believe, because of some linkage of the kind I have described in this logic of pain with what is past. It is rather that the past is somehow not taken seriously enough. It is taken into account but in far too limited a way. What is most troubling about guilt is its focus on some specific past wrong and the righting of it. Thinking in terms of guilt alone too easily locks one into an endless round of hurt done, hurt felt, hurt made up for.

All the while one must wonder, "is not there something more to be said, something more to be done, something more to be achieved?"

After still another hurt done her, after still another pain felt and shown, he says, "I'm sorry; forgive me; it won't happen again." She responds, "I know you feel rotten about it; I know that you are sorry, but frankly I've had all I can take of your indifference and your guilt because of your indifference and your pleas for forgiveness because of your guilt; it's been the same thing time and time again." We understand and sympathize with this woman and, perhaps, too, with the man. We wonder, "has the man chosen too easy a way out; does the logic of guilt, within which he feels and acts, channel responses in a way that leads to his avoiding what he must face in his past if the hurt to others and himself is to diminish, perhaps vanish?"

Something in this man interferes repeatedly with the love he has for the woman and interferes, too, with the love he would like to be able to have for himself. He is constantly racked by feelings of guilt. He may be perplexed by his feelings and his conduct. We can guess that he shall remain perplexed until he shifts his gaze from the particular wrong and the making up of it to wider and deeper patterns, patterns that once grasped allow him to see how, for example, what in his past with another woman explains his feelings and conduct toward the woman in his present. "Why," he may ask, "do I do these things, these self-defeating things?" and with this question stimulated by his suffering and the suffering of the woman he loves, he may be revealing a willingness to assume an attitude of greater respect for what has past than was shown when he felt guilty and sorry. But this broader, more serious view of the past and its linkage with the present may reveal, too, that he is taking more seriously who he presently is and who he will be. This question, "Why do I do these things?" may signal a concern with fundamental change rather than with restoration.

Part of what happened in the past of this man, we might guess, part of what accounts for what he now does and feels—the hurt done and felt, the emptiness—is guilt, a guilt pushed out of mind, but a guilt that nevertheless explains. If this guilt can be faced and its manifold connections with self-defeating patterns of feelings and conduct understood, the man, seeing things for what they are, might be able to relinquish them; and with this change he may bring about a transformation in his attitudes. For if his present life is dissatisfying—and nothing has quite the capacity to make it so than feelings and conduct derived from an unacknowledged guilt— we can suspect that time rushes on for him, and the end of his life is made more proximate and terrifying. But with freedom from self-imposed and unnecessary pain one travels some distance toward achieving satisfaction in the present and thus defeats somewhat the dominion of death over one's present life, both in the form of dissatisfaction with life and in the fear of its end.

But in this struggle to understand and to relinquish what makes for defeat in life, it is impossible for a man to travel far alone, for while pain felt in being as we are is our ally, the way of change is tortuous, and there is much within us that works against success. Love for others and for ourselves conditioned our earliest feelings of guilt; love for ourselves and love from others can help release us from its crushing effects. John Wisdom writes:

> We may hurry away and drown the cries that follow from those silent places—drown them in endless talk, drown them in the whine of the saxophone or the roar from the stands. Or, more effective, we may quiet those phantasmal voices by doing something for people real and alive. But if we can't we must return, force the accusers to speak up and insist on recognizing the featureless faces. We can hardly do this by ourselves. But there are those who will go with us and, however terrifying the way, not desert us.[1]

NOTE

1. John Wisdom, *Philosophy and Psychoanalysis* (Berkeley and Los Angeles: University of California Press, 1969), p. 282.

4 Shared Guilt

It is those that cannot connect who hasten to cast the first stone.
                              E. M. Forster, *Howard's End.*

FATHER Zossima's brother in *The Brothers Karamazov* says to his mother, "Little heart of mine, my joy, believe me, everyone is really responsible to all men for all men and for everything. I don't know how to explain it to you, but I feel it is so, painfully even. And how is it we went on then living, getting angry and not knowing." These are richly suggestive, troubling, words. Their precise meaning may elude us and we may yet have a sense of their profound significance, a sense that beneath them lies insight that cuts through to something essential about the nature of morality and human beings. We shall, I think, feel most at ease with the claims that we are responsible *to* all men and *for* all men, for they immediately suggest familiar claims about morality—the one, that a wrong we do to any man is something for which we must answer to every man, the other, that we have moral duties to others by virtue of their humanity and not some other fact about

Reprinted from *Wisdom: Twelve Essays* (Oxford: B. H. Blackwell, 1974).

them, for example, their sex or nationality. These claims are, of course, worth examining. But clearly it is the claim that "we are responsible *for everything*" that is most difficult to understand, that is most intriguing; and it is therefore this claim that most interests me. It seems clear that our attention is to be focused upon responsibility for what is seen as evil and not for what is seen as good, but where do we go from there? This essay is a record of my attempt to flush out its meaning and to come to grips with the truth there might be in it. I begin by setting out a number of rather likely responses to the claim that we are responsible for everything. I then consider separately several different lines of argument that might be offered in its support. I conclude with an assessment of the claim in the light of the responses there have been to it.

When we read the words "everyone is responsible for everything," we may be perplexed, as perplexed for example, as when for the first time we come upon the view that material objects do not exist. Can anyone really believe that you and I are responsible for everything, even those things of which we have not the least knowledge? Are we responsible for all that which, had we known of it, we should have done what we could to prevent? After putting such questions to ourselves we may be prepared, without much additional reflection, to judge that nothing intelligible is meant by such persons. We may feel that, while words are used with which we are familiar, persons who say such things do not—they cannot really—believe what it is that the words convey.

There will be those, of course, who respond to the claim that we are responsible for everything with no perplexity at all. They admit to understanding it by judging it to be obviously false. There are those things for which we are and those for which we are not responsible, and it is clear that we cannot be responsible for most of the things that have gone on, are going on, and will go on. People who take this line seem to have a firm grasp of when it is that a person is responsible for something. They evaluate claims of responsibility by appeal to a model of responsibility which we may label "individual responsibility" or "personal responsibility." This model has a hold on many persons and it is worth bringing out its characteristics, at least briefly, without further delay. This can best be done by noting typical ways in which responsibility is denied by some person for some occurrence where the occurrence is acknowledged to involve harm to some human being.

First, a person may claim that he was not involved at all in some harm's coming about and that it was another who was responsible. Second, a person may admit a causal connection between his body and some occurrence, but nevertheless deny that he was responsible, for he may argue that the movements of his body were not under his control or that he was unconscious when the movements took place. Third, a person may deny responsibility in what came about by questioning the existence of a causal connection between his admittedly voluntary conduct and the occurrence. Thus, if he were to stab what he took to be a live human being and the knife were in fact entering what had only seconds before become a corpse, he would not be responsible for killing a human being. Fourth, the result which has come about may be one that would not have come about but for the individual's conduct and still, if the result were only remotely connected with the conduct or if it came about too accidentally or because of the intervening act of another human being, there would be no responsibility for the occurrence. What lawyers might call "proximate cause" seems essential, then, for responsibility. Finally, to conclude this bare sketch of an elaborate mode of life, a person might admit that he was responsible for some harmful occurrence and reject the appropriateness of his being blamed or *held* responsible, for he may argue that he was without fault. That is, he may argue that his conduct met standards for proper conduct in the circumstances. On this view of the matter to properly be held morally responsible for some harm requires a causal and proximate causal connection between a person's faulty conduct and some harm. Now, if this is the model that we have—perhaps only vaguely—before our minds when someone says that "we are responsible for everything" we naturally think that what he says is false.

We may react to the view that "we are responsible for everything" in still another way. The claim may strike us as similar to other claims that appear to be straightforwardly about the world but which, as we soon discover from the array of defenses presented for them, really involve modification of the concepts that enter into the claim. We may come at this view of what is going on in the following way. Imagine, we might say, a man who felt guilty over suffering by anyone, anywhere, and at any time. He would seem to have feelings appropriate to the belief that he was responsible for everything. But this man would remind us of those with whom we are already familiar, perhaps even remind us of ourselves, persons who feel guilty in circumstances where it is inappropriate to feel that way and about whom we say, "they suffer from neurotic guilt." But the inappropriateness in neurotic guilt is not merely the result of the fact that a person believes something to be so about the world that is not. It is not, for example, that the man feels guilty over having killed someone and his belief is erroneous. In such a case we say to him, "Look, relax, you didn't kill him and you ought not to feel guilty about doing so." Learning of his mistake the man may cease to feel guilt over the death. But the neurotic would react differently. He appreciates that he hasn't killed anyone and he persists in feeling guilty, so he tells us, over the person's death. Here we may believe that the inappropriateness of the feeling ties in with a restructuring of the conceptual links between fault, responsibility, guilt, and feeling guilty. Well, if something conceptual is afoot with neurotic guilt, what shall we say of "we are responsible for everything" a claim which, if taken seriously, would lead to feelings of guilt of the most astoundingly neurotic kind?

If there is conceptual revision, it does not appear to be such a modest revision of one or more moral concepts as is going on, for example, when someone says of sexual intercourse without love that it is prostitution and of sexual intercourse with love that it is chastity. The claim seems to imply a revision in the concept of responsibility which is incompatible with the very idea of morality, for moral offenses seem preeminently ones in which the conditions of fault obtain.

If conceptual revision is involved it appears to have still another feature. "We are responsible for everything" has a partner at the other extreme: "None of us is responsible." These claims, at opposite extremes, may be regarded by some as involving not just revision of concepts central to morality but a shift that empties these concepts of usefulness. With these claims, as with "all of us are mad" and "all of us are selfish" we may be impressed by the lack of consequence of contrary cases. Everything is accommodated by the proponent of these views. But if we are responsible for everything, surely, an objector will argue, there is no longer any service being performed by the concept of responsibility. There is no point to our having the concept, for distinctions captured and thought important are erased. It is one more case where insulation from refutation is purchased at the too great price of informativeness and usefulness.

There are, then, these typical philosophical responses to the putting forward of a paradoxical claim: "nonsense," "false" and "empty." But there are other responses which reveal that considerable indignation is aroused by the claim. The view is surely put forward with the suggestion that it is an advance in moral thinking, that insight is being provided and that desirable moral conduct will follow acceptance of its truth. But is it not simply a mistaken moral point of view, one that has evil implications? Is it not a return to a morality, if we should be willing to call it that, beyond which we have advanced? Does it not remind us of what Ezekiel found unacceptable?

> What mean ye, that ye use this proverb
> concerning the land of Israel, saying,
> The fathers have eaten sour grapes,
> and the children's teeth are set on
> edge? As I live, saith the Lord God,
> ye shall not have occasion any more
> to use this proverb in Israel.

> The soul that sinneth, it shall die.
> The son shall not bear the iniquity of
> the father, neither shall the father
> bear the iniquity of the son: the
> righteousness of the righteous shall
> be upon him, and the wickedness of the
> wicked shall be upon him.

We may feel indignant, then, for what is morally false is put forward as morally true.

In fact, the claim that we are all responsible for everything, particularly when tied to narrower cases, say, being told that as whites we are responsible for the condition of the black man, responsible even for the evils perpetrated before our birth, produces not just intellectual disagreement, not just critical analysis but unquestionably, in the case of some people, considerable anger, sometimes anger of such intensity that we may become suspicious and wonder what nerve the claim has touched. There may be various reasons for this anger. Many of us feel already weighted down with guilt where normal conditions obtain, and it is understandable that we should not appreciate the suggestion that the magnitude of the burden be substantially increased. There are also those who see any claim leading to expanded responsibility and inevitable feelings of guilt as merely increasing the amount of breast-beating and bemoaning what is past, a looking backward that increases suffering but does not attend to the tasks before us.

Finally, there are those who believe they have the right to judge others and they become disturbed by views that make questionable the exercise of their right. In fact, they are as angered by the view that no one is responsible as by the view that we all are. For they think responsibility, guilt, and blame important concepts and believe that often others and not they are responsible and should be blamed. But if we are all responsible, or if none of us is, then it seems as if we are all precluded from blaming. "Judge not lest ye be judged." Anger may be aroused, then, for feelings regarded as legitimate are blocked and do not have the outlet they now have.

It is clear that the claim "we are responsible for everything" may anger us and that even more limited claims about our responsibility, when we think we are innocent or perhaps when we wish to hide our guilt from ourselves, will arouse anger. But I think that for some persons it will be a troubled anger. We know too well that the paradoxical reveals the hidden. And underlying our bewilderment, our anger, even our contempt, may be a feeling that these recorded responses to the claim that "we are responsible for everything" are inadequate, and that some insights not yet revealed underlie the claim.

There is something else that may add to the uneasiness some of us feel, even after all objections are put forward. We have feelings that we do not reject so quickly as we reject feelings labelled "neurotic guilt," and yet they seem to be feelings no less at odds with certain moral criteria. For example, a man may take pride in the accomplishments of his countrymen when all he appears to share with them is his nationality. A black man may feel pride where before he did not because of his beliefs about the accomplishments of other black men, ones who lived before he was born. And do we not feel shame and think it appropriate, at least sometimes, over actions of our country with which we have not been involved? Again, to think of Jews as a class may bring to mind a mode of thinking we abhor and that led to unspeakable horrors. But may not the Jew think of himself as different and take pride in his being different? Here, then, there is a sharing and an experiencing of an emotion that people may not react to with the anger and vehemence characterizing the claim about responsibility and what are taken to be its implications for being and feeling guilty. Why should this be?

I started with a claim that not even the man putting it forward felt capable of explaining. Some of these objections brought to light that this claim has the power to arouse strong emotion. And it evidently does this because, being a moral claim, it seems to have implications for the kinds of persons we are, the conduct we should and should not engage in, the feelings we should, but do not, have. And now, as I see it, the ground is laid for seeing what features of our moral life may have led persons to make this claim.

II

One man, out to kill another, succeeds by stabbing the man to death. He is tried, convicted and punished for murder. He is responsible for the man's death; he is adjudged guilty of murder. Another man, with precisely the same state of mind, engages in precisely the same acts, but by coincidence the man into whom he has thrust his knife has, unknown to the actor, died seconds before of a heart attack. About this would-be killer, we would not in the law, or indeed in everyday judgments outside the law, say that he was responsible for the man's death; and in the law he is not *held* liable or responsible for the man's death though, on some theories of attempt, he would be guilty of attempted murder. But were we convinced that the man did all that he believed necessary to kill, I think we should be tempted to make the following moral judgments: he is guilty; he is as guilty as if he had succeeded in killing; and, finally, we might also be tempted to say of him that morally he is a murderer or, at least, no different from a murderer. Students of the criminal law are familiar with discussions that deal with punishing less severely the man who attempts and fails through some fortuity than the man who succeeds. It is clear that a major problem posed by the differential punishment of attempters and consummators is the apparent lack of a moral difference between the two classes of men.

I want now to draw some distinctions relevant to the theme of this paper, several of which have been stimulated by thought about this case of attempted homicide. First, we shall want to keep separate, though they are obviously related, the concepts of responsibility for harm and being held responsible or blamed because of some wrong or offense. When a person is responsible for harm this ordinarily implies a causal relation between that person's actions and some harm. When a person is held legally responsible, this ordinarily implies the decision to impose a generally recognized deprivation upon the person because of some defined wrong. Similarly, when a person is blamed, a negative attitude is expressed toward the person because of some wrong. The law sometimes permits persons to be held responsible even though they are not responsible for harm, witness the case of being held responsible for attempts. And, of course, we all the time blame persons though they have not succeeded in causing harm.

The second distinction is that between being responsible for something that has occurred and being responsible for the performance of some task in the future. The one is retrospective; the other is prospective. Consider, for example, this passage from Freud:

> Obviously one must hold oneself responsible for the evil impulses of one's dreams. In what other way can one deal with them? Unless the content of the dream (rightly understood) is inspired by alien spirits, it is a part of my own being. If I seek to classify the impulses that are present in me according to social standards into good and bad, I must assume responsibility for both sorts; and if, in defence, I say that what is unknown, unconscious and repressed in me is not my "ego," then I shall not be basing my position upon psychoanalysis, I shall not have accepted its conclusions and I shall perhaps be taught better by the criticisms of my fellow men, by the disturbances in my actions and the confusion of my feelings. I shall perhaps learn that what I am repudiating not only "is" in me but sometimes "acts" from out of me as well. (*Collected Papers*, V, 156)

The retrospective responsibility urged here by Freud is clear. The prospective responsibility is to deal with the dream material as one's own and not as something alien to one. Indeed, the entire analytic process can be seen as a subtle combination of these types of responsibility, for it requires for success a person's assuming responsibility for change and this is partly, at least, dependent upon recognition of one's retrospective responsibility for the way one is.

The third distinction is that between being responsible in the sense of being morally liable to answer or respond, equivalent to being guilty, and being held responsible. Many persons are morally answerable for wrongdoing without being in fact held answerable.

There is, next, a distinction between "being guilty *of*" and being a guilty person. Being guilty *of* does not admit of degrees. One is or is not guilty of some wrong. But being a guilty person does admit of degrees. We think, for example, that other things being equal, a murderer is more guilty than a thief, that, other things being equal, one who intentionally kills is more guilty than one who kills negligently. Now if we examine our attempter and consummator, there is a temptation to say that, while they are guilty of different offenses or wrongs, they are equally guilty persons, that the upshot of their conduct does not bear on their degree of guilt. On this view, what is determinative of the degree of guilt is the state of mind with which a person acts and the value of the interest he threatens. But this line of thinking fails to distinguish sufficiently a person's blameworthiness and a person's guilt, both of which admit of degrees.

Let us turn to our attempter again. Suppose that a moment after he stabs what he assumes to be a live human being he is overcome with remorse and with feelings of guilt. Then he discovers that he has not killed the man. We can imagine a sigh of relief. The blood is not on his hands. The remorse vanishes. He does not feel as guilty, that is, the intensity of the pain associated with his guilt feelings is lessened and this reflects a recognition on his part that he is less guilty. Why is this so? To be guilty is, among other things, both to owe something to another and to be the justified object of their hostility. But what we owe, what we must do to make amends, is a function partly of what has actually been done. And the hostility that people feel is partly determined by the hurt they have actually suffered. So, the fortuity of not having killed puts our attempter in a position where he arouses less hostility and where he has less to do to make amends. He is, to be sure, still guilty—for reasons I shall soon go into—but his guilt is less than that of the consummator. Both are, however, equally blameworthy, for our moral assessment of their characters as manifested in their conduct does not treat as relevant the fortuitous upshot of their acts.

What is the relevance of all this to the claim "we are responsible for everything?" First, the claim, quite clearly, should not be interpreted to mean that all persons are causally connected with all evil deeds and all harm. Second, the claim should not be interpreted to mean that all men are guilty of each and every offense that has been committed. The phrase "for everything" should be understood as meaning "for all types of wrongs, harms, evils"; it does not mean, then, that we are responsible for every instantiation of the type. Third, the point of the claim is that we are all responsible in the sense of being morally answerable for or guilty with respect to every type of wrongdoing. Now why are we all in this position?

Let us consider just the value of human life and wrongs related to it and let us look again at our last step attempter. He is as blameworthy as the man who kills. He is also a guilty person. But this carries the proponent of the claim that we are all responsible for everything only a short distance. For, while the man causally disconnected from death in my example may be guilty and as blameworthy as a murderer, it is simply not true that all men stand to the death of human beings in the same relation as men who have done all in their power to kill and who have only failed through some fortuity. What is true of these men is that they intend to kill; they do all in their power to kill and only some fact irrelevant to moral judgment of their persons, say, some unknown intervening agent or unknown circumstance, distinguishes them from the man who kills. But it is precisely these important facts that make these men guilty and that distinguish these men from most of us. And so examples of men doing all they believe necessary to kill hardly touch most persons, for an insignificant number of men fit the description of those who have done all they believe necessary to kill. It might be granted, then, that if "we are responsible for everything" is interpreted as I have interpreted it, and if the world were composed entirely of persons such as our attempter, the claim would be true. But the world just is not that way.

Let us consider, next, a man who intends to kill, who takes substantial steps towards killing and who then abandons his project because he fears being caught—the man he seeks to kill is guarded by the police. How does he stand legally and morally? In the law he is generally treated as a man who has attempted to kill and his abandonment is not a defense. Such a case does not satisfy even the proposed liberalized abandonment rule of the American Law Institute's *Model Penal Code*, for the man cannot be said to have "voluntarily renounced his criminal project under circumstances manifesting renunciation of his criminal purpose." And it seems clear that if the man is one who held back primarily or solely because of fear of apprehension, there are no marks to be placed on the credit side of his moral ledger sheet. It may even be claimed that "in the eyes of God" he is indistinguishable from the last step attempter. Suppose just for the moment that this claim is granted. Those who hold out against the claim "we are all responsible for everything," now interpreted as "we are all guilty," will still find it an exaggeration for, while the class of those who have intended to kill and who have taken substantial steps toward this end and then turned back out of fear may be larger than the class of those who have gone the whole way, few additional persons, hardly all of us, fit into this class of attempters.

The class of the guilty widens considerably when we consider a man's character and what he desires to do. Suppose that a man desires to kill. Suppose he firmly believes that were he to possess Gyges' ring, with its capacity to make him invisible, he would kill. All that holds him back is fear. Is he any less guilty than the man who turns back at a later stage because of fear? It is precisely here that we can imagine the proponent of our extreme view pressing forward. The man has not formed an intention to kill, but his reasons for restraint are not morally creditable ones and he is not, just because of a decision not to proceed, excluded from the class of the guilty. Indeed, morally, does such a man differ from the killer? If he does not, is not the class of those who must admit to sharing the guilt associated with murder enlarged considerably?

We have travelled some way from our killer and our last step attempter to the man who desires and turns back out of fear alone or, for that matter, any reason that is not a morally creditable one. If we believe that all such persons are guilty and if we accept as warranted the view that most, if not all human beings, do on some occasions desire to kill, desire, indeed, to do a range of acts that constitute harm to others, and that it is a rare human being who has always, given such desires, restrained himself for morally creditable reasons, then we shall perhaps find the claim, as so interpreted, more plausible than before. This is, I think, one possible line of defense for the view "we are all responsible for everything" and it needs now to be evaluated.

To begin with, someone may suggest that there is a significant moral distinction between, on the one hand, the class of those who do everything they believe necessary to succeed and those who succeed, and on the other hand, classes ranging from the substantial step attempter back to those who merely desire and do not form the intention to kill out of fear. What is true of the latter classses and not the former is that, if we are dealing with free agents, there is always the possibility that, were such persons to continue and the policeman no longer around, they would turn back for morally creditable reasons. Let us call this change of mind for morally creditable reasons "a change of heart." Now, if we grant that a change of heart is possible, even in the case of a man who firmly believes he will go on to kill, we cannot say, and the man who himself has the desire or even the intention cannot say with certainty, that he will take steps to kill and that no morally creditable reason will bear on him and lead to a change of heart. Indeed, we cannot even say this about all those individuals who do all that they believe necessary to kill, for, in some cases, they can by subsequent conduct intervene and prevent harm from resulting. The person who has poisoned a cup of coffee can empty it before it is drunk.

The merit in this suggestion is its drawing our attention to differences in degrees of guilt. The claim "we are all responsible for everything," at least on the basis of the kinds of cases we have been considering, should not depend on the truth of "we are all equally guilty," for we are not. But the suggestion I have set out is neither clear nor, on either of two possible interpretations, correct in the explanation offered for differences in degrees of guilt. Is it being claimed that the mere possibility of a change of heart makes one less guilty than one who has not had such a change and who has gone the whole way? But why should a possibility bear on one's guilt? We are tempted to say at this point, "It's only if he in fact will have a change of heart that he is less guilty than one who has not." But perhaps then the claim is that the person might be as guilty; it is just that neither we nor he can know whether or not he is. This position seems wrong too, wrong because it fails to give sufficient weight to what a man has actually done. A man's going farther simply makes him more guilty than one who has not gone as far even if the one who has travelled less distance will in fact not have a change of heart. With each step one takes toward the ultimate end an opportunity to forbear is left unseized and more guilt is added, the quantum of stain increasing as one moves to the end. It is not the absence of a change of heart but the distance travelled that bears on guilt. Neither the last step attempter nor the consummator has had a change of heart, yet they are not equally guilty.

Let us now consider those classes of persons about whom we can say "They have accepted desires to do acts that are wrong." As I employ the concept of accepting desires these are either persons who form intentions to realize their desires or, if having desires, they do not form such intentions, fail to do so for reasons that are not morally creditable. Are such persons guilty at all? What do we think of such persons? What, too, we may ask, do they themselves feel and for what reasons? We think of them, I believe, as guilty, at least to some degree. And it is clear, I think, that persons who accept desires may feel guilty because of their mental posture.

What might account for and justify one's having a feeling of guilt with respect to a state of mind in circumstances where harm to another is not evident? Freud's explanation is that the infant equates the intention or wish with the deed because of its belief in the omnipotence of thought. One may also be reminded of Jesus' remark that the man who lusts after a woman has already committed adultery with her in his heart. Jesus here is, I think, closer to the truth than Freud, for there is reason for guilt with respect to desires and intentions apart from a primitive belief in their causal efficacy. It is important to see that certain mental states are in themselves destructive of valued relationships. They are destructive because the relationship is partly defined in terms of feelings and thoughts.

Consider a man who has a valued relationship of reciprocal trust and fidelity with his wife. Now suppose that this man at some point forms the intention to commit adultery. If the man commits adultery and the wife learns of it, we can readily see the harm to her. But suppose the wife does not learn of the husband's infidelity, for there has been none. She only learns of his intention. Here too we can see harm. But suppose she doesn't learn of his intention. The relationship has still been damaged, for it is defined partly by each partner being prepared to exercise restraint out of love and respect for the other. The man's intention reveals that he is no longer prepared to abide by this condition. It is understandable, then, that he may feel guilt, understandable that, after a change of heart, he may wish to confess what he desired to do, what he formed the intention to do, in order thereby to restore a relationship he sees himself as having damaged.

To be sure, our relationship to others in society is only rarely that of love or friendship. It ought however to be a relationship, and responsible persons so understand it, in which there is reciprocal care and trust and respect. A man who accepts a desire to do an act harmful to another has a state of mind incompatible with a relationship among human beings that is valued by all responsible persons. He is, given his state of mind, no longer trustworthy; and his state of mind reveals a lack of care and respect for his fellow men. Certain states of mind constitute wrongs, then, for these states are themselves incompatible with morally required relationships between human beings.

Now suppose that we have all been guilty of such wrongs. Suppose we have harboured malicious intentions. What are the consequences? Is this guilt which we have all shared one for which it is possible to make amends? If we have by our thoughts separated ourselves from this ideal, only partially realized, community of responsible persons, how do we atone, how do we become *at one with* that community again?

Let us turn attention first to those who have accepted desires to do acts harmful to others but who might yet have a change of heart. Their guilt implies, I believe, the assumption of responsibility, a prospective responsibility, to renounce their desires and to labor toward being persons who, in caring for and respecting others, are themselves worthy of the care, trust and respect of others. The significant point is that a relationship of a valued kind has been ruptured by a state of mind; it can be restored by the person acquiring the appropriate state of mind.

What, however, of the man who goes the whole way? There are those in this class who succeed and those who fail. Let us first compare those who fail with the class of those who intend and who take substantial steps in furtherance of their intention. It is a mistake, I believe, to treat, as the American Law Institute's *Model Penal Code* would have it, these different classes of attempters in the same manner. The man who intends and who takes substantial steps has ruptured a relationship. He has also, perhaps, increased the risk of an actual invasion of the specific interests of other human beings by his steps in furtherance of his intention. But when we deprive such persons of their liberty, it is not primarily as punishment for wrongdoing, but as a preventive measure. Punishment in such cases does not perform its essentially moral task of restoration. A person's apologizing and renouncing his criminal purposes would be sufficient to restore his relationship with others. If he does not renounce his criminal purposes, preventive reasons can explain his continued incarceratino, but it is not the case that a deprivation is being visited upon him for wrongdoing and that with this deprivation he pays off some debt to society.

It is otherwise, I believe, with the man who has done all that he believes necessary to realize his criminal purpose but who fails. He has ruptured a relationship of trust and respect for which he might make amends in the manner I have described. But he has done more and he owes more. Punishment of such a man is peculiarly appropriate, for it deprives him of any unfair advantage he has acquired as against all responsible persons in society. The picture I have in mind is as follows.

There are rules in all societies compliance with which provides benefits for all persons. These benefits consist in non-interference by others with what each person values, such matters as continuance of life and bodily security. Making possible this mutual benefit is the assumption by individuals of a burden. The burden consists in the exercise of self-restraint by individuals at a point where, were they not to exercise it, others would in the normal course of events be harmed. If a person fails to exercise self-restraint even though he might have, he relinquishes a burden which others have voluntarily assumed and thus gains an advantage which others, who have restrained themselves, do not possess. This system is one in which the rules establish a mutuality of benefit and burden and in which the benefits of non-interference are conditional upon the assumption of burdens. A moral equilibrium is, then, established.

Our man who goes the whole way but who fails through some fortuity upsets that equilibrium, for he has relinquished a burden which others have assumed which is a condition for the benefits of the system. He resembles the consummator in this respect, but he differs from the attempter who might yet turn back. This attempter has decided to relinquish the burden of self-restraint that is the condition for the benefits of the system, but he still has opportunity to exercise restraint. He doesn't as yet have, as does the man who goes the whole way, the unfair advantage that justice demands be taken from him. The man, then, who goes the whole way derives the benefits others do not; by relinquishing a burden others have assumed, he gains an advantage over them. Punishment, a deprivation occasioned by wrongdoing, deprives him of his advantage and restores the upset moral equilibrium.

What accounts for the differential punishment of the two classes of men who do all in their power to succeed, the unsuccessful attempter and the consummator? I suggested earlier that they were equally blameworthy but not equally guilty. The consummator owes more because he has taken and acquired more. He has not just the satisfaction attendant upon relinquishing the burden of self-restraint, but he has the satisfaction attendant upon realization of his desires. He has not only upset the equilibrium I have described but violated the rights of particular persons. He must then do something to reestablish the moral equilibrium resting on mutual exercise of restraint and he must do something to make amends for the particular harm to the individual.

There is one final matter that I want to raise before we move on to other types of cases that may be appealed to in support of the claim "we are responsible for everything." So far, I have sought to loosen up objections to the claim by interpretations of responsibility, blameworthiness and guilt. It is particularly important, however, to avoid too cramped a concept of what we are guilty of. It is clear that focusing, as I have, upon essentially legal examples of attempted homicide and homicide, has its disadvantages. The law has good reasons for attempting to define offenses in relatively precise terms. But, of course, in doing this and in being guided by other principles that define the law's proper scope much that is evil is not encompassed within the law. Murder, legally, for example, requires a corpse and what enters into defining a corpse are physiological considerations. But morality is not limited in this way. There is a death in life, and when we look upon ourselves, our acts and our thoughts, few, if any of us, can escape the taint of blood. Nietzsche writes: "One has not watched life very observantly if one has never seen the hand that—kills tenderly."

III

Thus far I have attempted to bring out one way in which it makes sense, and might even be true, to talk of our all being guilty, our all sharing in guilt. I want now to turn to another class of cases where more is involved than our each sharing certain states that give rise to guilt. The individuals I want now to consider are labelled in law "accomplices." Part, I believe, of what underlies the claim "we are all responsible for everything" is the view that we are all in one way or another accomplices in evil. This line of argument at some point dovetails with the one we have just examined, for persons may be guilty because of intentions which, if executed, would make them accomplices.

In these cases of shared guilt, it is acknowledged that there is an individual who is guilty of some wrong. In the law he is labelled "a principal." One shares the guilt associated with that wrong because of a relationship to the principal. There is a considerable body of legal material on complicity. Let us first turn our attention to this.

As our law is now constituted, one who counsels, advises, or persuades another or who aids another in committing a crime is a party to that crime and since the abandonment of common law distinctions between principals and accessories, guilty of the same offense as the principal and subject to identical punishment. Encompassed within the law governing complicity are the following classes. First, there are those who advise or persuade another to commit some crime and who are parties to the crime without being causally connected with the ultimate harm. Complicity doctrine is not the ground of liability when a responsible actor gets an irresponsible person, say a child or insane person, to perform some deed that is contrary to the law. Likewise, if one gets a responsible person to perform an act proscribed by law either through coercion or deception one is directly related to the offense and once again complicity doctrine is not the basis of liability. There are, second, those who aid or assist another in the commission of a crime. The law generally requires that the person's purpose be to assist in the commission of an offense, though there is strong difference of opinion within the United States' Federal Courts whether or not knowingly facilitating the commission of an offense should be sufficient. The law, for example, will generally leave untouched the businessman who provides a commodity which he has good reason to believe or even knows will be used for a criminal purpose if the businessman can establish that he was indifferent to the commission of the crime and was just interested in his usual profit. New York, going further than has generally been the case, has created a new offense titled "criminal facilitation" in which liability requires: (1) a belief that "it is probable that" one is rendering aid to a person who intends to commit a crime, (2) that one engages in conduct which provides such a person with means or opportunity for the commission of an offense, and (3) that the person has in fact aided another to commit a felony. There are, next, those who aid the perpetrators in escaping detection, apprehension, conviction, punishment. There are other classes of persons which legal systems have sometimes singled out and treated as guilty, usually not of the offense committed by the principal actor, but of separately defined offenses. These include: those who knowingly profit from the wrongdoing; those who stand by and do not make an effort to prevent the offense when they might have done so without risk to their own well-being; those who fail to take steps to prevent escape. The law leaves untouched those who merely approve and those who create by their conduct the general atmosphere in which crime thrives. This is a sketch of the legal situation with regard to complicity. What are the boundaries of moral complicity?

First, I have so far in this essay limited myself to the states of mind of desire and intention. But it is important to realize that a person may be blamed for matters which he neither desired not intended to bring about. One may, of course, be guilty of reckless or negligent homicide. One may be blamed for taking unwarranted risks. I raise this point now, for it is apparent that the law generally circumscribes liability for complicity by insisting upon purpose or at least knowledge. Legal liability is not imposed upon the man who aids another but does so recklessly or negligently. Those who wish to impress upon us our complicity in wrongdoing will wish, and correctly I think, to take into account a variety of states of mind that, associated with conduct, are a basis for guilt.

Second, they will move to expand the concept of complicity so that it encompasses all conduct for which one may rightfully be blamed that substantially contributes to wrongdoing. Thus, individuals may seek to bring out possible sources of our complicity in wrongdoing by bringing to our attention: unwise and repressive legislation which requires restraint over powerful impulses without any clear corresponding gain to society, the unwillingness of citizens to provide greater financial support for educating the young and educating and compensating the police, for improvement of prisons, for greater numbers of probationary officers, for improved facilities and programmes for juvenile offenders; they may point also to those many aspects of our culture that convey to persons generally an impression of indifference and positive distaste for the values of human affection and respect; they may point to all that leads to frustration, anger and discontent and that might be otherwise if people were less afraid and prepared to sacrifice more. The list is obviously long that enumerates the many things we do and fail to do that contribute to the existence of wrongdoing. Unless we are saints are we not guilty of involvement in at least some forms of conduct that promote wrongdoing?

Third, one may share guilt because one profits from wrongdoing. There are clear cases here, cases in which we believe that a person partaking of the results of some wrongdoing thereby associates himself with it, as when one accepts known stolen goods from a thief and uses them for one's own satisfaction. What is not clear is that we are all guilty with respect to all types of wrongs if this is the basis of our guilt. I turn now to one final point that may support the view that we all profit from wrongdoing of every kind.

It is important, I think, in coming to appreciate our subtle and not so subtle complicity in wrongdoing to understand what psychological investment we may have in it. This requires that we take into account a possible connection between shared guilt in the preceding section and shared guilt through complicity. What I have in mind has been much elaborated upon in psychoanalytic literature and in Sartre's richly textured *St. Genet*. The criminal crosses a barrier which others desire to cross but do not. He gives in to impulses; others restrain themselves. This process involves a heavy cost in satisfaction for each person and is accomplished through the internalization of precepts and negative responses to their violation. Set up in us is a mechanism which aggressively responds to threatened and actual violations. If something like this is so, we can conjecture that the criminal services our needs in the following ways. First, he acts out what we only fantasize. We can derive satisfaction from identification with him. We can derive satisfaciton from seeing our desires realized if only through the medium of another. Second, the criminal, while a vehicle for our satisfaction, among other things, also arouses envy and anger in us toward him. He has seized what it has taken us so much to forgo. Normally, we must forbear from expression of anger; we must not strike out but rather keep the aggression in. The criminal is someone, however, if only in an institutionally governed way that we can strike out against and regard it as acceptable. Here, we may say, our instinctual life is relatively unhampered. Third, the criminal also permits the aggression that otherwise would turn inward to be deflected outward. He, not we, is guilty. Finally, he perhaps services us in still another way. In giving in to what we all desire, he manifests what we too often do not, power and daring, a willingness to risk oneself for the satisfaction of strong desires. Both Stendhal and Nietzsche, among others, believed that criminals demonstrated that there was still a spark of life left in man.

If there were no criminals, should we have to invent them? If there is truth in the suggestion that we should, how much of human conduct is subtly devised to perpetuate the very existence of those of whom we say we are so longing to be rid?

IV

There is another class of cases where we may speak of "shared guilt." These cases do not support the view that "we are all guilty with respect to all types of wrongdoing." They do support the view, however, that we are all guilty of some evil. In Camus's *The Fall* the hero walking along the bridge hears the splash and does nothing. His guilt is apparent. It is here that pressure will begin to be applied by the proponent of the view that we are all guilty. How are you and I to be distinguished from Camus's hero? Are not you and I, in the lives we lead, omitting to do what we could to prevent suffering? Perhaps people in need are not within a few feet with their suffering vividly before us. What difference should that make? How shall we go about distinguishing between the child starving close by and the one starving in some more distant place? And shall we distinguish between a hand held out for food and one held out, perhaps less apparently, for compassion and understanding? I think that it may be admitted that if we could in fact prevent suffering and do not then we are responsible for it. But, it will be argued, this does not mean that we are at all blameworthy or that we have any guilt with respect to what comes about. We all have obligations closer to home and perhaps, if we each attend to these, more in the end will be gained by all. Also life has more to it than attempting to rescue or assist those in need. We have also our own lives to lead at some level of intensity, joyfulness and beauty. A concept such as "what can reasonably be expected of one" may be used to block the claim that we are guilty because we fail to prevent suffering we might have prevented. The concept of guilt is linked to that of fault and this concept is in turn linked to demands that may rightfully be placed upon man. These in turn connect with the reasonableness of a man's conduct. And it may be argued that it is at least not unreasonable to act in ways that are not related to alleviating suffering. There is some balance we must all strike. So the argument will go.

In response, this may be said. It is clear that there are those persons who have sacrificed more than we. When we reflect on their lives, if we are sensitive and honest, we may be struck by our weakness and selfishness. At this point, people may begin to be genuinely troubled over their moral condition. First of all, which one of us can say that he has always done what could even reasonably be demanded of him? Have we balanced in an acceptable way living a decent human life and helping those who are less fortunate? The grip of the claim "We are all guilty" tightens here, for it is no easy matter to determine where the line is to be drawn when a concept as vague as "reasonableness" is our guide; and we may, naturally, feel anxious, when drawing it, that we have unwarrantedly favored our own interests over those of others.

Second, even if we have done all that could be expected of a reasonable man, perhaps there is still more that we could have done. I think of these remarks of Jaspers in The Question of German Guilt:

> When our Jewish friends were taken away, we did not go out into the street and cry aloud until we also met our death. We preferred to remain in life for the weak, even if justifiable, reason that our death would not in any way have helped. It is our own fault that we are still alive. . . . It demands that we should take on us the consequences of being alive in such conditions.

There are two types of situations that Jaspers presents to us in his book that he does not clearly separate. There is, first, the case of our failing to do whatever we can to prevent evil. There is, second, the case of one who has not necessarily failed in any way, but that person is guilty merely in remaining alive when others have their lives unjustly taken. An attachment to human solidarity, were it not for our weakness, would lead man to sacrifice his life though this would accomplish nothing but an affirmation of human solidarity.

A person may certainly feel in either of these cases what he will label "guilt." And if in fact one has guilt for not doing all that a saint, a hero, an angel would do, then surely "we are all guilty" in this sense. But when Jaspers talks of fault and guilt in the circumstances in which he does, the idea of guilt, because fault conditions, normally associated with guilt, are absent, is merging into something else. He recognizes this by labelling the guilt "metaphysical guilt." I think this phenomenon may also be described as "self-guilt" or "guilt before oneself" or perhaps best "shame."

Its striking feature is that being metaphysically guilty does not imply a rupture in established moral relations with others. Thus nothing may be re-established by confession or repentance or forgiveness or punishment. Guilt, in standard cases, is linked to the idea of an imbalance occasioned by some wrong. A relationship with another or others has been damaged. It connects with ideas such as fault, restoration, confession, making amends, repentance, forgiveness, punishment, justice, excuse. It is all otherwise with shame. Fault is not essential to shame; we do not make amends for a shameful act. Nothing can be forgiven. Punishment is inappropriate and cannot serve as it does with some types of guilt to restore relationships.

There are two points that seem to me particularly important to emphasize here. First, in failing to do the extraordinary, we may feel that we are less than we would desire to be. Still, it is inappropriate for others to make any demand on us to have performed in that way. Second, our failure may be, not in neglecting to do the extraordinary, but in doing and failing to do things that, while ultimately involving harm to others, are most directly crimes involving ourselves, crimes that consist in one way or another in failures of integrity, failures to be and to act as our conception of ourselves dictates. There is a strong temptation to talk of guilt here—guilt before ourselves—rather than shame, for fault conditions do obtain in many instances, and it is our own choices that have turned us away from being ourselves. The impulse to talk of shame, in this type of case also, as in cases of not doing the extraordinary, comes from the inappropriateness in these cases of alleviating the feelings we have by conduct such as confession, making amends, asking forgiveness or receiving punishment.

V

We have looked at cases where there may be talk of guilt and we had before us the extraordinary, and there was a temptation understandably felt to say that guilt and shame were there merging. We have also looked at cases where guilt may be spoken of and a rupture in a relationship with others is not involved but rather a break with one's self which gives rise to an obligation to return to or be what we believe we should be. In all these cases, whether the act we think of is one within the capacities of normal men or whether it calls for some extraordinary conduct, it is an identifiable individual who possesses in some sense a capacity to have behaved otherwise and has not. This partially accounts, I think, for the temptation to talk in these cases of guilt though, as I have tried to show, in some instances the concept is being stretched. There are cases, however, in which the pull on the concept of guilt is very severe indeed and where shame seems far the more appropriate concept. In these cases we feel shame for what others do where none of the reasons for sharing guilt so far brought out seem apparent.

What are the criteria for taking pride in and feeling shame over the deeds or characteristics of others? We connect ourselves in some way with others and when they act we see it reflecting not just on them but on us. They may be at fault and thus guilty. We are not at fault, but we still see their conduct as reflecting on us, reflecting perhaps on deficiencies we share with them. We want to hide from the view of others because we believe that what another person has done reflects on us because of our connection with this person. Suppose my own son does well; I may take pride in his accomplishments. If he does poorly, I may feel ashamed. There is here, we want to say, my involvement with what he is and, thus, how he performs partly and understandably reflects credit or discredit on me. But is it always this way? And when it is not, where one's efforts do not link up in some way with those of others, is taking pride or feeling shame irrational? Something like neurotic guilt?

There are always bases for identifying oneself as being a member of a certain class, a thing of a certain kind. There are, for example, a variety of criteria relating to identifying oneself as a male, as an American, as a Catholic, a kind or selfish person, a human being. In identifying ourselves as human we think of characteristics we have that other animate things do not. We might think that to be human is to be rational or have the capacity for rationality. Or struck by the significance of the setting forth of values and what this implies, someone may identify being human with the capacity to feel guilt. When such a person comes upon a psychopath he may feel a strong temptation to describe such a person as an animal in the body of a human being. We look upon ourselves as members of a class, and there are usually relatively well-accepted bases for so doing—though the criteria are, as in the case of "human being" or "person" numerous and complicated in character. Now, this is the reason why, when a member of a class of which we consider ourselves a member does something commendable, we take pride. It is in the family so to speak. It is saying something about us. And likewise for the ignoble. There is something, I think, to the feeling of being ashamed at being human when one reflects on the horrors perpetrated by our species and likewise for the pride in its accomplishments. One would rather be an animal when one hears sometimes of what mankind is capable of. One shares in the attributes manifested in some evil deed. If animals judged us, we should turn away in shame at what humans have done to them.

When Father Zossima's brother said "we are all responsible for everything" we may feel that he was struggling to make some point about the appropriateness of our feeling shame, perhaps before God, because of the evil done by any human being, as if some defect in us were revealed by what any human being did. But I think what he found impossible to explain was our all being in fact guilty and as guilty as any wrongdoer who had ever perpetrated evil. It is not that what another does reflects upon us. It is that we are in fact the other. Mankind was a unity, a single child of God, and there was no separateness, the act of one being the act of all. He saw close connections to the point of a moral identity where we see significant disconnections. At the heart, then, of "we are all responsible for everything" is a metaphysical belief about persons and actions similar to beliefs we ascribe to certain primitive societies which interpret the act of one member of a tribe as the act of each and every member of the tribe. Father Zossima's brother extends the unity of the family against which Ezekiel rebelled to the whole of mankind. And the implication of this, for him, is that any moral judgment of one by another makes no sense. Why did he come to these beliefs? Was it because of a sense that there was evil within us all and that its manifesting itself in time in the acts of one person rather than another was essentially adventitious?

"We are all responsible for everything." I have attempted to see how understanding might be furthered by examination of several different types of consideration that might lead to the claim. I first moved to interpret "responsible for everything" as "guilt with respect to all evil." I next drew a distinction between being guilty and being *as* guilty. I then traced various routes to a view that we are all guilty. One route emphasized the commonality of impulses toward evil. Another stressed the degree to which we are all implicated in wrongdoing through complicity with others. Another stressed guilt arising from our failure to act. Still another attempted to draw attention to guilt before ourselves.

Interpreting the claim as I have, what should our attitude be toward the objections raised at the beginning of the paper? A number of the objections are wide of the mark because "responsible for everything" is erroneously interpreted as implying some causal connection between all persons and all harm. When the claim is interpreted as "we are all guilty" a number of criticisms may be deflected.

It might still be argued, however, that "we are all guilty" deprives of usefulness the concept of guilt. I do not think that this criticism is valid. First, as we have seen, there are still degrees of guilt. Second, gaining an insight into our own moral condition may lead us to assume responsibility for becoming different, for becoming persons whom others can understandably care for, trust and respect.

5 Lost Innocence

Eve looked upon the tree of knowledge of good and evil and saw that it was good for food. It was pleasing to her eyes, and she believed, because of the serpent's words, that eating of it would make her wise. My own reactions to the tale of Adam and Eve resemble those of Eve to the tree. My attention has been fixed upon it; it has charmed me; and I have come to believe that reflection upon it has the potential for furthering—if not wisdom— at least understanding of what it is to gain knowledge of good and evil and to lose innocence.

This is an essay stimulated, to a considerable degree, by reflection on this single case, one so assiduously examined by untold numbers of religious thinkers and comparably neglected, as is the subject of lost innocence itself, by philosophers. Of course

I am indebted to Professor David Sachs, whose response to an earlier version of this paper at the Oberlin Philosophy Colloqium in the spring of 1975 has assisted me in thinking more clearly about the subject.—H. M.

my aim is not exegetical. I use the tale simply as a springboard for philosophical inquiry. There are pitfalls in this way of proceeding. As I see it, the principal of such is the temptation to have eyes for this case alone and no other, supposing that because it is a rich story, it is the only one. It remains only, by way of introduction and for whatever exorcising power it might have, to express the hope that in my case the serpent did not intervene, that the truth in the saying "pride goeth before the fall" has sunk in. I must confess to a serious doubt whether this is so when I sense the profundity and complexity of the tale and subject and the serpentine nature, at times, of my reasoning.

You will recall that Eve succumbs to temptation; Adam joins in disobedience; and each appears then to experience what is, arguably, the first peculiarly human and painful emotion alluded to in the Old Testament. "The eyes of them both were opened, and they knew that they were naked; and they sewed fig leaves together, and made themselves aprons." Adam and Eve feel before each other shame, the shame earlier referred to in the passage, "and they were both naked, the man and his wife, and were not ashamed." But this chilling, and from a certain perspective, appalling mythic moment clearly presents more than an instance of shame before another; and this is so for at least two reasons. Adam and Eve experience shame, but they also suddenly acquire a liability to its experience; they are, as of a moment, possessed of a sense of shame. In addition, upon eating the fruit of the tree of knowledge of good and evil both Adam and Eve acquire knowledge of good and evil and grasp that they are naked. With this they lose their innocence. As the fruit manifests its magical powers, then, Adam and Eve acquire a sense of shame, experience a loss of innocence, and standing before each other, experience shame before each other. This essay deals only with lost innocence. It may be viewed as an attempt to analyze Eve's experience immediately upon eating the fruit of the tree but before she had observed Adam or observed Adam observing her.

When Adam and Eve disobeyed God, they are commonly said, though neither expression is used in the tale itself, to have "fallen" and to have lost their innocence. In what sense or senses might they no longer be innocent? In disobeying God each was, if one accepts that they were required to obey, guilty, in an attenuated sense, of, at a minimum, disobedience, and being guilty of this, they were no longer innocent of wrongdoing. Being guilty and no longer innocent in this sense, however, does not seem to imply, given their child-like nature at the time of disobedience and their ignorance of good and evil, moral culpability in disobeying. In the act of disobedience, then, there was moral innocence. And any vices manifested in this act would also have been those of innocent persons. In eating of the tree, however, each acquired knowledge; and it is this knowledge, not the fact of their disobedience nor any moral culpability in disobeying nor the presence of any vice in disobeying, that must in some way account for their losing innocence.

To further fix these points in our minds, imagine Adam and Eve commanded by God not to eat of the tree of life and imagine them then disobeying. They would no longer be innocent of wrong-doing. They would be, however, innocent as this state contrasts with knowledge, for they would not have acquired knowledge of good and evil. Young children are, of course, often precisely in this condition, for they are often guilty of wrongdoing, indeed they may feel guilty, while still retaining their innocence. Imagine, next that God had not forbidden them to eat of the tree of knowledge of good and evil; imagine then Adam and Eve eating the fruit of it. They would have lost their innocence, but they would not have bene guilty of any wrongdoing in doing so. There is, then, innocent conduct, conduct that is either not wrong or, while wrong, not something for which the individual has any responsibility. There is morally innocent conduct, conduct that is wrongful and for which one is responsible but in the performance of which one manifests no moral culpability. And there are innocent persons, persons who are absent a certain kind of knowledge. As I shall use the expression, then, an innocent person is not innocent merely by virtue of being a person not guilty of wrongdoing or not morally guilty of wrongdoing, but a person absent a certain kind of knowledge. It seems clear that it is in acquiring this knowledge that one *loses* innocence rather than simply no longer *being* innocent because one is guilty or morally guilty of wrongdoing.

We have now to ask what is the character of the knowledge that accounts for this loss? This question opens up two large areas of inquiry. First, there is an epistemological inquiry into the manner in which the knowledge is acquired and into the basic logical features of this knowledge. Second, there is an inquiry into the special objects of the knowledge and how knowledge of these objects manifests itself. I commence with the first inquiry.

The knowledge Adam and Eve acquire of good and evil first reflects itself in their learning of their nakedness. "Their eyes were opened and they saw they were naked." What can be made of that? They come to know something about themselves; and we have to ask, once we determine in which way, whether it tells us anything important about our subject.

Their eyes being opened contrasts with familiar classes of cases in which one comes to know something. We may be looking for some object, say a watch that is, unknown to us, beneath some apples in a fruit basket. We lift several apples and now know what we did not before, the location of the watch. The mode of acquiring knowledge in our tale is different—different, of course, because what is unknown appears, from the language of the tale, to have been before them all along. Nor does their mode of acquiring knowledge resemble those cases in which attention is averted to a feature of a situation all the time before one to be seen that has not before been taken in. It is not as if their situation were like one in which we say to a person, who fails to note a feature of a painting before their eyes, "Now look more carefully and you'll spot the nut shell under the table," and the person looks more carefully and exclaims, "Of course—how could I have missed it—it was staring me in the face." To be sure, once the eyes of Adam and Eve were opened their attention may well have been fixed upon features of a situation that lacked this magnetic power before, but it is reasonable to suppose that they perceived before and after their loss of innocence the same perceptual aspects of the situation.

Clearly, too, the knowledge in their case is not come at through use of any deductive procedure as if we were to imagine Adam and Eve putting two and two together and reaching the appropriate conclusion. Hardly. Nor is their situation precisely like that philosophically exploited example in which a figure is drawn in such a way that one looking at it may say, "Now I see it as a duck" and "Oh, now I see it differently; I see it as a rabbit." The case of lost innocence, Adam and Eve's coming to see themselves as naked, is different, for what they would report seeing before and after their acquisition of knowledge would be the same. The knowledge that they are naked, then, is not derived from literally opening their eyes, or paying more careful attention to physical features of their situation, or drawing some deductive inference from what they already know, or aligning differently perceived aspects of a situation already before them. All this seems obvious.

With these unlikely candidates ruled out, the stage is set for the following possibility. While the word "knowledge" is used and while the familiar metaphor of coming to know something—the eyes being opened—is also used, and while knowledge of a certain kind is commonly associated with losing one's innocence, loss of it really consists in nothing more than a different way of feeling about what has been before one all along. Nothing new is learned; something new is felt about what is already known. Perhaps the following example may illustrate this conception of lost innocence. There is a musical piece; one is aware of each element, the relationship between each of the elements, and the whole. There is nothing that has escaped the person. Now, as of a certain time the piece pleases. With time there is a change and there is now an experience of displeasure. We are familiar with the feeling of having "grown-up" musically when, for example, our tastes change and Bach, let us say, replaces Tschaikovsky in our favor. With this change we are to imagine no new truths grasped. With lost innocence, so the suggestion is, the situation is similar. Whereas one had earlier felt at ease, felt a kind of natural joy, one now is cursed with an absence of joy, perhaps more, with feeling anxious and bad. Wordsworth's lines perhaps capture this: "Yet I know, where'er I go, that there hath past away a glory from the earth." This suggestion, because of its emphasis on feelings, is a move in the right direction, but it is, nevertheless, mistaken in discounting entirely the role of new knowledge. We do not believe that Adam and Eve merely feel differently about nakedness. We think that their feeling differently is intimately connected with their coming to learn something. And this is, of course, abundantly clear with lost innocence generally; it is not reducible to a different way of feeling.

The following model might then be suggested: a wine bottle is filled half-way; a person initially describes it, perhaps because life generally has been viewed as disappointing, as half-empty. Life improves; optimism supplants pessimism; and the bottle is now described by the same person as half-full. There is a temptation to say of such a case that no new truths have been grasped, that there is only a re-description, to which one is attached, accounted for by a shift in attitude. The new description does, however, connect what is before one in each case with a different class of things; it resembles, then, the case in which we first see a figure one way and then another way. Is it false to claim that the person's knowledge has been increased in such cases by appreciating the appropriateness of the new description? I do not think so. If this is accepted, the case comes closer to capturing the character of the change that occurred with Adam and Eve, for, after they eat of the fruit and acquire knowledge of good and evil, they grasp matters in a different way, in a way intimately related to a shift in attitude that is expressed in their new understanding.

But this still will not by itself do if the picture before us is merely that of a new description of a perceptual situation expressive of a new attitude. This is so because it is a special feature of the knowledge Adam and Eve acquire that it enables them to see through appearances to reality. One could grasp connections of matters already before one, already available for reflection and not requiring further empirical investigation, without believing that one had grasped a reality lying behind appearances. The case of the wine bottle is of this sort. The innocent, however, move about in a world absent of a certain significance for them; their world is opaque. Essentially connected with lost innocence is an acquired disposition not to accept things at face value. The reality hidden from the innocent Adam and Eve, however, was not hidden as our watch was hidden beneath some apples. It is rather that what is the real character of what is already before them is not appreciated. The following example may serve to illustrate this point. Imagine a person gazing at an early Sienese painting in which there is depicted a town in the upper right hand corner of the painting and a road leading from the town and on this road, at some distance from one another, three figures resembling, but different from, each other. One could take all this in and describe the painting quite accurately in terms of these details and yet fail to realize, fail to understand the language of the painting, if one did not appreciate that space was being used to depict the passage of time, that this was, in fact, a painting depicting stages in the life of a single saint. To look upon the painting as one of three different persons on a path would be similar to the innocent Adam and Eve's way of viewing the world; looking upon what is before one and grasping its significance would resemble one essential ingredient of what is present in the loss of innocence.

On this interpretation, their eyes being opened to their nakedness becomes a species of insight. Indeed, is it not evident that both could have been blind and had, in the requisite sense, their "eyes opened" to their nakedness? There is a distinction between the knowledge that makes possible the eyes being opened, the knowledge being gained by the opening of the eyes, and the visual observation of their own and the other's nakedness once they are possessed of knowledge. Seeing themselves as naked reflects seeing something about themselves and of themselves in relation to the other and the other in relation to themselves that had before escaped them and having feelings and attitudes appropriate to this new knowledge. Their loss is, then, of something essentially connected with gaining something, unlike, for example, the loss of a loved one and more like the loss of peace of mind accounted for by acquiring anxiety.

The knowledge of their nakedness in the tale, because it is a species of insight, comes at a stroke. The scales fall from their eyes. It is a salient feature of lost innocence that it can be lost instantaneously. Consider this passage from Henry James' *The Portrait of a Lady*, describing, I believe, a moment of insight and a loss of innocence:

> "What have you to do with me?" Isabel went on.
> Madame Merle slowly got up, stroking her muff, but not removing her eyes from Isabel's face. "Everything!" she answered.
> Isabel sat there looking up at her, without rising; her face was almost a prayer to be enlightened. But the light of this woman's eyes seemed only a darkness. "Oh misery!" she murmered at last; and she fell back, covering her face with her hands. It had come over her like a high-surging wave that Mrs. Touchette was right. Madame Merle had married her. Before she uncovered her face again that lady had left the room.

When Adam and Eve eat the fruit, the knowledge they acquire of nakedness is also knowledge of an object the character of which was unimaginable to them prior to the acquisition of the object. Adam and Eve are unable to set out to lose their innocence with a clear idea of what it is that they will lose and what it is that they will acquire. Eve is seeking to acquire knowledge of good and evil and to gain wisdom, but these are surely words without meaning for her just as God's threat of death must have been perplexing to Adam.

There appear several reasons for this. First, Adam and Eve possessed neither the requisite concepts for interpreting experience nor a grasp of the applicability of the concepts to relevant cases. Their innocence is like that of the young child who unconcernedly goes about nude. The adult's disturbance at the child's nudity meets with the child's perplexity, not the perplexity of "how could anyone hold such silly views!" but a perplexity that derives from not understanding the concepts used by the adult. I assume here that at least two kinds of cases are imaginable. In the one there is an absence of the concepts of good and evil; in the other there is a failure to take in that a concept applies to a particular range of cases. Secondly, an essential requirement of lost innocence is experience of a certain kind. Here the explanation for Adam and

Eve being incapable of imagining what they would acquire is that experiencing the thing in question is a condition for imagining it. The attempt to explain to Adam and Eve what it is to be naked in the requisite sense would be comparable to explaining pain, without in some way causing it to be experienced, to a person who had never experienced it. In the tale, insight into their nakedness gives the requisite experience.

These features of lost innocence also explain, in part, the unanticipated quality of their experience. The discovery at the heart of their lost innocence differs in its logical character from that made, say, by an early voyager who finds an island for which he has been searching. We could, of course, imagine the voyager acquiring some unanticipated truth. Oedipus, for example, is determined to discover the killer of Laius and without anticipating it—let us so imagine—discovers that he is the man for whom he has been searching. Oedipus is like a voyager who finds his island in a place other than he expects. But while in Oedipus' case and that of Adam and Eve what is acquired is unanticipated, there is an essential difference related to their sudden acquisition of concepts. Oedipus already has a clear idea of the class of things that would satisfy the hypothesis he has formulated; and his surprise comes from its being a certain member of that class, a member other than he expects. With the child and Adam and Eve to formulate the hypothesis would itself mean having the concepts which their innocence belies their possessing.

There are several additional features of the knowledge they acquire. It is not about the world generally but a narrower range of matters, but about this narrower range, there is a belief of a general kind. The objects of the knowledge embodied in lost innocence are human beings. The loss of innocence may be occasioned by what one learns about oneself, about oneself in relation to others or about others in relation to oneself or to third parties, human or otherwise. Adam and Eve both have a new view of themselves and of the other; both are acquainted with their own and the other's nakedness. Next, the knowledge is not merely about matters in relation to human beings but knowledge gained about the nature of human beings as persons of a certain kind with relations of a certain kind through their mental states and conduct to what is of value. There are several points here: first, coming to believe that human beings are mortal, where before one held the belief that some at least were not, is to learn something about human beings, something that may shatter an illusion and account for loss of one's naiveté, but it is not—so it is my understanding of the concept—to lose one's innocence, for natural death comes to us independent of our own conduct or the conduct of other human beings; second, when one loses innocence one has a belief about the nature of persons occasioned perhaps by a belief about some particular motive or intention or action, but it is a belief that is not restricted to these particulars; third, one has a belief about human beings, not in any special role or as performers of some special task, say, as fruit pickers, but human beings as *persons* in relation to things of value; fourth, loss of innocence is often a matter of degree, a degree that is partly a function of the generality of one's belief. One's innocence is still largely intact if the belief one holds is restricted to a belief about oneself; it is entirely intact if it is about just one other person. If, for example, one came to see something, and indeed to see and feel something about just one other human being as a person of a certain kind, say that the person was manipulative in dealings with others, but kept to all one's former feelings and attitudes and beliefs about all others, one would not yet have crossed the threshold of innocence. One retains innocence, too, if the awareness one has of others is not applied to oneself. There are forces at work that may block one's knowledge from extending beyond a particular or restricted range of cases. We may think, for example, of a person as no longer innocent. We now experience some perplexity that innocence is revealed by the person to us about some matter. We may revise our former opinion and think, "he is still to a considerable degree innocent"; we may think this is so with a vague idea of powerful motives at work attaching one to innocence; and we may then search for the particular explanation for its retention, operating on the assumption that what is natural is the extension of the knowledge of all relevant cases. A person might be knowledgeable enough to know that all humans are mortal, that he is a human being, and yet reveal to us that in his own case it is different, that at most lip-service is being paid the universal generalization and that there is one notable exception. We are familiar with this case and similar ones are presented in the area of innocence. It is this feature that may account for the loss more often being occasioned by a discovery about either oneself or about those close to one. Adam and Eve ideally illustrate this. The more impersonal a relationship, the easier it is, when innocence is involved, to isolate one's discovery. Thus, one more easily retains innocence when confronted with certain relevant truths about strangers than friends. The general belief connected with lost innocence does not, however, arise through a process of generalizing from particular cases. It is not, for example, as if one comes to believe something about oneself and then notes similarities between oneself and others and generalizes. It is rather that, knowing about human beings, one comes to grasp the presence in their world of certain elements; and one's responses reflect an awareness of these elements in a special way.

When one loses innocence one has, then, an awareness of others and oneself and of possible relations between persons that one did not before possess. The manifestation of the loss in the case of others and oneself differs. In one's own case there is self-consciousness in at least two senses. First, one is an object for oneself, and there are judgments one now makes about oneself that one did not before make. What allows for these judgments of the self is the acquisition of concepts and the capacity to apply them to oneself. The child has desires and acts, and the ways in which it does are expressive of the nature of the child. When innocence is lost there is a view of oneself as having a nature that had before merely expressed itself. Secondly, lost innocence is characterized by self-consciousness in a different sense a sense captured by the imagery of Adam and Eve covering their nakedness. For reasons yet to be stated, but essentially related to the first kind of self-consciousness, one becomes less natural, less spontaneous; hesitancy enters one's life. One thinks before one acts, and, as it were, adjusts a mask before making an appearance. One acts as if the self of which one is now conscious were vulnerable.

There is a need now to pause. The tale of Adam and Eve may be acknowledged to be an example of lost innocence. It may even be granted that several of the features of their loss of innocence have been fairly accurately set out. There may still be, however, an uneasiness stemming from a sense that there are losses of innocence and losses of innocence. Most concern will focus, I believe, on the connection of insight with lost innocence.

The tale does depict, I believe, a moment that may properly be described as a moment of insight, and this moment corresponds to the moment when Adam and Eve both lose their innocence. But we may naturally wonder what significance there is in this fact. The creation story itself collapses into a few days what may well have taken slightly longer to achieve. And the myth of Adam and Eve eating the fruit and thereby acquiring knowledge of good and evil surely collapses into a moment of startling illumination and disorientation what must have been a gradual process in the development of the human race and, for that matter and more to our purpose, so it may be thought, its development within any single individual.

Further, there are two interpretations—at least two—of Adam and Eve's situation, and I have been proceeding as if there were only one, the one supportive of the claim about insight, and disregarding the other, arguably, equally plausible interpretation which may cast doubt upon it. I have been assuming that when Adam and Eve acquired knowledge of good and evil they had an insight into what was true of them all along, namely that they were naked. On this interpretation their nature was fundamentally the same before and after they acquired knowledge. With knowledge they made a discovery and did not suddenly become different persons except insofar as they possessed a knowledge not before possessed. Imagine a child that has come to understand the propriety of wearing clothes in certain settings; imagine that child now laughing at another child who goes about naked in those settings. Our no longer innocent child believes that the innocent child does not yet know what is so. But there is another possible interpretation of our tale, and it may capture something about loss of innocence particularly as we apply it to sexual maturation of the human being. This interpretation would claim that the concept of nakedness has a different significance in the tale before and after Adam and Eve eat the fruit. When they do they both acquire knowledge of good and evil, but they also instantaneously become, not just knowledgeable but different and not different because they know what they did not before. They had an immediate awareness of this difference because of their knowledge. They make a discovery, but they do not have an insight into what was there before them all along. Nakedness before they eat represents their innocence, the innocence of their acts and motives; nakedness after they eat represents the fact that their motives of action in relation to each other have undergone a fundamental transformation. Lust enters their lives coincident with disobedience and with knowledge. With the young person in the sphere of sexuality the situation may appear similar. There is a knowledge of what is permitted and what is not. There are changes in the character of one's desires, feelings, fantasies, and dispositions with maturation, and one is conscious of oneself as disposed to do what is not permitted. One here loses innocence gradually, learning something about oneself that might not have all along been there to know. This kind of case is not one that fits the model of lost innocence as involving a moment of illumination into something that has all along been so. Some response to these points is required.

First, the tale can mislead if it suggests that the acquisition of the knowledge of good and evil, the acquisition of the capacity to apply these concepts appropriately, something that is an essential component in any case of lost innocence, is an instantaneous achievement. I have wished to keep separate the knowledge of good and evil and the knowledge of nakedness; it is the latter knowledge that involves insight though the former knowledge is essential to it.

Second, Adam and Eve are in a state of total innocence prior to their eating the fruit and after they do, their innocence is lost. This may give the impression that innocence is an all or-nothing affair and it is not. An adult may, unlike the child, for example, possess the concepts of good and evil and still retain innocence but not an innocence as thoroughgoing as the child's who lacks the concepts. The adult may have gone a considerable way toward losing innocence and then something happens and we are prepared to claim the threshold has been crossed, innocence lost, as if one were gradually losing one's grip and then finally lost it.

Third, is insight common to all cases of lost innocence? Think of Isabel and Madame Merle. There was a moment of illumination in which Isabel took in the truth of Madame Merle's betrayal. There was insight here. But suppose Madame Merle had simply told her "My dear child, I've married you; and what I've done is no different than what countless others have done and are each day doing." Suppose that Isabel believes her. We might agree that she has learned about the world and that, without any insight on Isabel's part, she has lost her innocence. I am inclined to say that Madame Merle's words would have occasioned Isabel's loss of innocence only if she had provided Isabel with an insight into human affairs and not just some empirical truth about human beings to which she was privy and Isabel not. I say this because of a sense that the innocent are blind to what is there before them to be seen. In Isabel's case, unlike Adam and Eve's and the very young child's, there is an illusion, a false belief that things are better than they in fact are, but she is innocent because she, unlike Madame Merle, has not opened her eyes, nor was she disposed to, to what was there before her to be seen. I draw, then, a distinction between being simply ignorant of what is so and being innocent; being innocent in this respect resembles naiveté. All cases of lost innocence involve, then, coming to appreciate what is already before one. Still, while this is sometimes a matter of insight, it need not always be so. Loss of innocence is sometimes, perhaps most often, a gradual affair, for it is associated less with a sudden insight than it is with gradually realizing some truth.

Those who lose innocence think about themselves and others in a new way, in a way that essentially relates the loss to acquiring knowledge of good and evil. But what is it to come to know this in a way that defeats innocence? How is this to be made more precise? I am far from being sure; and I have, at most, some vague and adventuresome suggestions on this topic. Let us again turn to the tale. A suggestion might be this. There is in the myth a dramatic presentation of two individuals instantaneously acquiring a sense of right and wrong, acquiring, that is, among other things, a capacity to apply principles of what is right and wrong, being disposed to apply them when the appropriate occasions arise and to feel certain ways toward oneself and others when appropriate, given one's beliefs about what is right and wrong. There are, I believe, several drawbacks to such a view of lost innocence.

First, it should be noted that there does not appear to be any logical connection between Adam and Eve covering up and their recognition of the wrongfulness of disobedience. Their covering up seems the opposite of an appropriate guilt reaction such as the disposition to confess. They cover their nakedness because they grasp a truth about themselves in relation to good and evil; and having grasped this truth, it would, among other things, have been shameless to parade before the other naked. Second, losing innocence is something, as I have argued, that can be lost instantaneously and thus something may be acquired instantaneously. But this does not appear to be so with acquiring a sense of right and wrong. Third, one can lose innocence through coming to know evil where this is not essentially related to what we should ordinarily think of as doing what is wrong. One may lose innocence by coming to know evil that is divorced from both evil motives and wrongful actions. Evil, for our purposes, can be thought of as anything for which human beings are believed responsible that in some way is destructive of what is of relatively great value. I mean to include cases of failing to promote what is of value, preventing its promotion and actually destroying what is of value. What would then account for some conduct being wrong would be the evil that it causes. Evil motives, intentions, conduct, results, persons—all would acquire their nature as evil becasue of a connection with some damage to what is of value. But evil, on this view, may be divorced from wrongful conduct. With the purest of motives, in the absence of conduct we should regard as reckless or negligent, one acts to help another in distress and in the attempt causes a worsening of the distress. One is responsible here for the distress, but there is no wrongdoing and no culpability. Again, we may feel compelled to produce evil in order to prevent a greater evil. An appreciation of these common, fixed and tragic features of the world of human conduct—one that calls to my mind Wittgenstein's early view that the world is independent of our will and that anything should happen as we wish is but a grace of fate— may be, in my judgment, an occasion for loss of one's innocence. We are no longer naive, no longer possessed of a false belief or of an illusion when we realize the limits of the human will, for example, the irreversibility of events and our inevitable deaths. We are no longer innocent when we realize those aspects of our world connected with the evil that humans are responsible for. Loss of innocence gives us a knowledge, then, not of what is right and wrong or the set of dispositions to act and feel in certain ways connected with this knowledge, but a knowledge of evil and the set of dispositions to act and feel that are connected with this knowledge. Loss of innocence, while presupposing a knowledge of both good and evil requires a coming to know evil in a certain way and cannot be restricted to coming to know good in a certain way. Finally, and most importantly, treating loss of innocence as essentially the same as acquiring a sense of right and wrong breaks down, for it appears that a person may have a developed sense of right and wrong and yet retain innocence. A person may know what is right and wrong; a person may know this in a way that implies dispositions to feel and act in certain ways; a person may, to a remarkably sophisticated degree, possess the capacity to state the reasons why certain conduct is right and certain conduct wrong; a person may be even philosophically sophisticated and possess what we may believe are accurate views on the nature of claims that some things are right and some things wrong, some things good and some things evil. All this may be so and the individual still innocent. But how can a person retain innocence, possessing all of these moral and intellectual capacities? What additionally is required? Several things.

The knowledge of evil must be by acquaintance, and it must be associated with certain attitudes and feelings. The insight to which I have been referring is fused with feeling, not contingently but necessarily so. First, then, a central strain of meaning in the concept of lost innocence is, as I have said, experience. This may account for sometimes saying, after learning of a person's loss of virginity, that the individual is now no longer innocent. It is precisely that strain that inclines some Biblical scholars to claim that Adam and Eve did not have sexual intercourse prior to eating the fruit. They did not "know" each other. But, as I see it, experience must be of a special kind for lost innocence; and sexual intercourse, by itself, is hardly sufficient for the loss. We can, then, safely allow Adam and Eve the pleasures of intercourse before they eat the fruit. With lost innocence the component of experience requires that one or more of several possibilities be realized. First, that one have been oneself the object of evil. In addition to being the object one must satisfy the criteria for knowing that one is. I think again of Isabel Archer. James writes:

> On the afternoon I began with speaking of, she had taken a resolution not to think of Madame Merle; but the resolution proved vain, and this lady's image hovered constantly before her. She asked herself, with an almost childlike horror of the supposition, whether to this intimate friend of several years the great historical epithet of *wicked* were to be applied. She knew the idea only by the Bible and other literary works; to the best of her belief she had had no personal acquaintance with wickedness. She had desired a large acquaintance with human life, and in spite of her having flattered herself that she cultivated it with some success this elementary privilege had been denied her. Perhaps it was not wicked—in the historical sense—to be even deeply false; for that was what Madame Merle had been—deeply, deeply, deeply.

Isabel explicitly characterizes the experience which she has had. It is possible, however, to have an experience of evil that will occasion loss of innocence without this explicit classification. Second, one may have, because of a capacity for empathetic identification, an experience of evil where others and not oneself are the objects. It is not that one merely sympathizes with others; it is that one experiences through a process of imaginative identification what is, at least to some degree, the experience of another. Third, one may have acquaintance with oneself as the subject or potential subject of evil; I understand this to imply experience of the evil that one may do. Unless one has this knowledge of oneself as the subject or potential subject for evil, some innocence is always retained.

But still what is it to have this experience in the requisite sense, the sense that will account for lost innocence? I have said that it is a knowledge by acquaintance; but what are the marks of this acquaintance? It seems possible to have the concepts of good and evil, to apply to oneself and others correctly these concepts, to be acquainted with evil, at least in a certain sense, and still retain innocence. One can, for example, in a childlike, innocent manner, submit to what one correctly believes to be evil and retain one's innocence. There understandably may be a temptation in such cases to say of such persons, "they do not really, despite what they say, believe in the existence of evil." The experience one has must be one that appropriately reflects the features of the object with which one says one is acquainted. What appropriately reflects the experience of evil?

It is an experience essentially related to painful experiences whether one grasps oneself as the subject or object of evil. Further, the pain of the evil itself is complemented—because one also has a knowledge of the good—by a pain derived from the thought of what might have been and was not. First, one cannot experience something as evil and not experience it as painful. Those who experience something as evil must reveal a fear of it, a disposition to avoid it, to recoil from it; it requires courage to stand one's ground in the face of it; and the mark of the depth of one's conviction of its existence in one's life and its seriousness is one's horror of it. One's sense of right and wrong reflects itself principally in indignation and guilt; one's sense of evil reflects itself in being abashed, appalled, horrified. If this is so, there is a conceptual not psychological oddity in the love of evil, for in manifesting such a love one would reveal that one experienced what one loved, not as evil, but as good. The evil man, the man who is said to love evil for its own sake, would appear, then, to love what is objectively evil, not what is evil for him. He must, though, if he is not to be an innocent evil one, have experienced evil. The Devil, to be truly malevolent, must have known evil before he became attached to the doing of it.

Second, loss of innocence is partly a painful experience because one now grasps what could have been the case and was not. One has a knowledge of good as well as evil. If we imagine Adam and Eve experiencing lust for each other and experiencing the other's lust for them, they are, whatever pleasures might also be associated with it, troubled, because of their knowledge and attachment to what is good, by at least two things: first, they are pained by a recognition in themselves of something they do not love but hate; and, second, they are pained by a recognition in the other of something in relation to them they hate and do not love. The pain, then, is to be viewed, as perhaps it most often is, with a vivid sense not merely of its constitutive components but its relational ones. There is an increment of pain just in the realization of what might have been and is not.

Third, the attitudes and disposition that are connected with the experience of evil are attitudes and dispositions that are themselves associated with painful experiences. These attitudes are nicely captured for us in the image of covering one's nakedness, a covering up that carries with it the burden of a calculating and cautionary posture. With loss of innocence we enter the world of trust and distrust and incline toward the latter; suspicion enters one's life. We are conscious of our vulnerability, both as we may be pained by what others do and we ourselves do and may do. Our guard goes up to protect us from the evil that we now believe may be done to us; and we cover up to hide from others and ourselves the evil we sense within us, that we may do and have done. The innocent lack guile. Animals and children instinctively behave in the face of threats as those who are no longer innocent behave in the face of evil. The responses of those who have lost innocence are, however, mediated by a belief in evil. Animals and young children are caused by features of their immediate environment to put up their guard, to flee; those who are no longer innocent possess a sense of the way things are that, independent of perceived features of a situation, lead them to take precautions. Matters that appear one way are appreciated as often being other than they appear; virtue may be vice in disguise. Part of what I understand by the Biblical saying "except that ye become as little children . . ." is related to these points as is the intensity of our satisfaction in the company of at least some children, nature, certain works of art, and those we love. All make less difficult an immersion in the immediate, a relaxation, a lowering of burdensome defenses and an opening of ourselves to satisfaction without distancing of ourselves.

The loss of innocence is itself sometimes thought to be an evil. It is not, however, the loss of some object which one had consciously valued and then lost. It is a loss of something that is only looked upon as a valuable once it is lost, and then, of course, its value may be exaggerated. With loss of innocence one acquires for this reason and others an historical sense. A powerful nostalgia may come into existence, motivating one to return to an imagined glorious state of being. The image of this state appears to force itself upon us with greatest intensity when evil is most present in our lives.

This leads naturally to the subject of recaptured innocence. There are individuals who may appear to have regained, at least in part, their innocence. Some attitudes and feelings we associate with the loss seem absent in their lives. Of course, a physical or psychological trauma may cause a return to a childlike state but with others it seems an achievement. Such persons—perhaps Socrates and Father Zossima may serve as examples—regain, without self-deception, some of their lost childlike innocence. This extraordinary achievement appears in their cases to come about through disarming evil, by overcoming what it is in one that accounts for the inclination to do evil and by overcoming, too, what it is that accounts for fearing the evil that might be done one.

Still, these are cases in which one might retain a vivid sense of evil in the world but only as it manifests itself in the affairs of others. There is, then, still an absence of total innocence. No doubt there are others, some mystics perhaps, who, having once lost their innocence, come with time to acquire the moral impregnability of Socrates and an outlook upon human life generally such that evil does not exist for them. A state approaching innocence is achieved through transcendence. They would, in their fashion, have regained innocence, but their state would still differ from that of the innocent child, for the condition they are in requires a journey that the child has, as yet, to make.

Innocence as purity, ignorance that is, of one's own capacity for evil, especially if conjoined with experience of evil in others, is bound to be an unsteady state. It requires that we not accept as a feature of our own lives what is recognized as a feature of the lives of others. No doubt, most anything is possible here, but the risk is always there that a moment of illumination will force upon one, what was forced upon David by Nathan, the truth, "thou art the man." Further, our conception of evil is still connected with earlier but surviving conceptions of defilement and contagion and for good reason. Even in cases where it is another and not we who have brought about evil, even in cases in which this evil is visited upon us, we may feel unclean. The explanation for this feeling is surely complicated. Evil, given the nature of human beings, has a generative power. It may summon to mind, though we have not done evil, that we are pleased that it has been done; and we then realize that we would have wished that it be done rather than not done. Again, it may stimulate in us a sense of our own desires to do to others the very things that have been done to us. Or again, evil is infectious, for the hurt we experience can give rise to rage and retaliatory impulses that seek expression to allay a sense of deprivation. And, of course, there is truth in the trite saying, regrettable as it might be, "misery loves company." Again, evil has the potential, when it is persistent and powerful in one's life to gain an ally in the person who suffers it. It then leads to an evil far worse than the evil visited upon one by others, the evil of a person's turning against life. Finally, because of the rage that it may occasion, it may arouse in us guilt and feeling this, we positively act to deprive ourselves of good for ourselves. Evil, like good, as it has often been observed, generates its own kind.

There are several important characteristics of evil that a focus on lost innocence forces upon our attention. First, evil is an element of human existence, manifested in various crude and subtle ways that makes for the destruction of what is valued. It has a unity and a unity conceived of as a force in the world. Pervasive features of human existence make for evil. Second, it enters our lives independent of our rational choice. We discover it before we choose to do it. The enemy is within before it can begin to be combatted. Third, because evil is viewed as destructive, we would not knowingly have chosen it. Evil is pictured as taking advantage of us when our guard is down; we are, in some way, duped. Finally, once it enters our lives, it has a generative power, and there are forces at work toward deceiving oneself and others as to its existence. All of this is nicely reflected in the tale by the serpent's duping Eve and Eve blaming the serpent and Adam blaming Eve. Thus the connection of evil with duplicity and blindness seems close. And this leads to connecting evil with the devil.

The devil—you will need no reminding—is the Prince of Lies. This appears so because evil is substantially promoted through ignorance as to its existence and nature. Two principal deceptions seem at work: first, that evil does not exist; second, that it alone does and the good does not. The denial of evil is similar to the denial of the devil. I find myself in agreement with Baudelaire. It is the work of the devil to deny his existence, for it contributes to the power of evil to believe it does not exist or, if it does, in others but not ourselves. It is natural that there should be the folklore that light frightens the devil and that he loves to work in the dark. Insight and constant surveillance gives him only an occasional opening. But, of course, among his other reputed strengths is subtlety and even insight and surveillance can be destructive. Life requires lowering one's guard. The other deception is the belief that the world is ruled by the devil, that our world is his kingdom. This is to accept despair as a way of life, or, rather, death. Here humans become accomplices in the greatest evil. Adam and Eve gain a knowledge of good and evil, and it is the good to which they are attached and which has the greater power.

The serpent's guile with Eve was no straightforward case of fraud. It is not as if he outright lied to her, promising her something he knew she would not get. He simply left out a few pertinent details of what she would get in addition to what he told her she would. He was a subtle salesman. There appears, for example, some truth in his telling her that she would gain wisdom. Losing innocence can hardly give assurance of this, but it seems a necessary condition for it. To appreciate that there is evil in the world, to hold to no illusions about it, to be serious about it, to have experienced its many manifestations, to have seen as well as evil what allows for its being overcome, to see all that makes for the good and to give it due weight—these seem among the essential components of moral wisdom. They link closely with lost innocence. It is surely this which partly accounts for the under- standable conflict that one might feel about God's command not to eat of the tree of knowledge of good and evil and about our longing for some imagined Eden. There is a good even in evil: the good that makes possible a life of a certain depth and scope. We operate with a conception of the worth of human beings that leads to our esteeming more highly those who are not just moral persons but morally wise persons. They have, in that profound imagery of the struggle between good and evil, not been crushed by what they have confronted, but have emerged, in ways mysterious to behold, victorious, capable, despite and because of knowledge, of affirming rather than denying life.